BODIES OF KNOWLEDGE IN PSYCHOSOCIAL PRACTICE

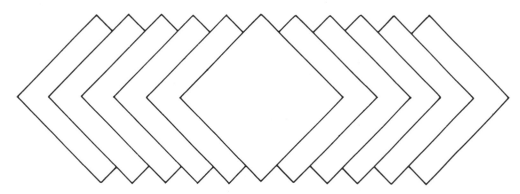

Roann Barris
Gary Kielhofner
Janet Hawkins Watts

SLACK Incorporated, 6900 Grove Road, Thorofare, New Jersey 08086

SLACK International Book Distributors

Japan
  Igaku-Shoin, Ltd.
  Tokyo International P.O. Box 5063
  1-28-36 Hongo, Bunkyo-Ku
  Tokyo 113
  Japan

Canada
  McGraw-Hill Ryerson Limited
  300 Water Street
  Whitby, Ontario
  L1N 9B6

Australia
  McGraw-Hill Book Company
  4 Barcoo Street
  Roseville East 2069
  New South Wales
  Australia

United Kingdom
  McGraw-Hill Book Company
  Shoppenhangers Road
  Maidenhead, Berkshire SL6 2QL
  England

In all other regions throughout the world, SLACK professional reference books are available through offices and affiliates of McGraw-Hill, Inc. For the name and address of the office serving your area, please correspond to

McGraw-Hill, Inc.
Medical Publishing Group
Attn: International Marketing Director
1221 Avenue of the Americas —28th Floor
New York, NY 10020
(212)-512-3955 (phone)
(212)-512-4717 (fax)

Editorial Director: Cheryl D. Willoughby
Publisher: Harry C. Benson

Printed in the United States of America

Library of Congress Catalog Card Number: 88-42960

ISBN: 1-55642-071-4

Published by: SLACK Incorporated
               6900 Grove Road
               Thorofare, NJ 08086-9447

Last digit is print number: 10   9   8   7   6   5   4   3

Introduction

Psychosocial practice involves the interface of people who hold different perspectives based on various bodies of knowledge. Sometimes this interface is harmonious. At other times the interface is conflicting, as when people define problems differently or when their views of their respective roles lead to disagreement. In either instance, professionals should appreciate and understand others' perspectives. At the same time those with a clear identity and commitment to their own professional perspective can more effectively contribute to the team and to patient care. The function of a team is, after all, to bring together people who represent differing ideas and abilities for the purpose of providing optimal health care.

Occupational therapists must both appreciate pluralistic viewpoints and have knowledge and expertise in their own field. The purpose of this book is to provide basic knowledge the occupational therapist must have to competently interact with other professionals and to selectively incorporate ideas and approaches into treatment. The text presents eleven bodies of knowledge that are prominent in the thinking of mental health professionals. These perspectives are covered so that therapists can know about them.

Our renderings of these bodies of knowledge are more absolute than what one typically encounters. However, our goal is to demonstrate a way to identify the many separate lines of thought that contribute to the ultimate configurations of ideas and actions in practice settings.

To facilitate comprehension of each perspective and to enhance critical comparison and evaluation of these bodies of knowledge, all chapters follow the same format. Each chapter begins with a discussion of the history and purpose of the body of knowledge. In this section, the following themes are generally covered: (a) how the knowledge emerged and what forces or influences led to its formation, (b) major writers or leaders who developed the ideas and concepts, (c) what fields or professions generally use the knowledge, and (d) particular features that make this body of knowledge interesting, noteworthy, and/or problematic.

The second section of each chapter, view of order, examines how the body of knowledge explains the well working of humans. The concept of health approximates what is meant by order, but it presupposes a particular perspective. For instance, some of the bodies of knowledge are not primarily concerned with health and illness. Thus, while they may not address health per se, they do present concepts about how human behavior is organized and influenced. The term order was chosen because it is broad enough to encompass many perspectives.

Each chapter then discusses disorders, or how the body of knowledge views psychosocial problems. Perhaps here more than in any other section the chapters portray the real differences in bodies of knowledge. How a body of knowledge defines a problem or disorder determines how it will attempt resolution. This is the topic of the discussion that follows next, action implications. Here, treatment techniques, a call for social change, or whatever action is prescribed by the body of knowledge is identified.

Two final sections of each chapter provide a perspective for critical evaluation. The criticisms and limitations section presents and interprets claims that have been made in the literature pertaining to the weaknesses or limitations of each body of knowledge. The commentary section addresses the body of knowledge from the perspective of occupational therapy, discussing its relevance and compatibility. This section offers an assessment of how the body of knowledge should be regarded by occupational therapists.

Needless to say, this chapter format worked more readily for some bodies of knowledge than for others. However, using this structure to organize the presentation of each body of knowledge served to highlight some of the gaps and inconsistencies as well as the strengths of each perspective. The themes of order, disorder, and action implications are of critical concern to any person working in the area of psychosocial dysfunction, and they must be properly balanced in any view. Thus, when a body of knowledge focuses on action without a clear formulation of order and disorder, or when disorder is concentrated on so heavily that order is relatively ignored, the body of knowledge can be said to be incomplete or lacking. Therefore, while our categories are imposed from without on each body of knowledge, this imposition facilitates critical analysis and evaluation.

The choice of certain words always presents a dilemma for writers; some of our choices bear mentioning. Every effort was made to eliminate sexist terminology throughout this volume. The terms "patients" and "clients" are both used throughout the text. Their use often reflects the context or setting being discussed. Thus, the term *client* was used in discussions of nontraditional situations, especially community mental health. *Patient* was used in discussions of more traditional medical circumstances. In addition, we used the term most often associated with the body of knowledge under discussion.

The term *psychosocial dysfunction* is used throughout the volume to refer to persons with (a) identified emotional disturbances, (b) mental retardation and (c) developmental disabilities or physical problems that have precipitated a psychological or social disturbance. In reality these categories overlap. All have in common a disturbance to psychological and interpersonal well-being. More specific terms such as mental retardation, schizophrenia, and the like were used when a particular topic pertained only to that subgroup of those with psychosocial dysfunction. Finally, we sought to avoid such terms as "mental retardates" and "the mentally ill," since such language does not acknowledge the human identity of these persons.

Each chapter contains a glossary and summary table as review and study guides. They also provide a ready means of comparison of different bodies of knowledge. Reference lists provide additional readings for the interested person. Our choice of references was based on the goal of using authoritative and representative works and is therefore not exhaustive.

Table of Contents

Bodies of Knowledge in Psychosocial Practice

Introduction   iii
1   The Medical Model   3
2   Classical Psychoanalysis   17
3   The Neo-Freudians: Adler, Horney, Fromm, and Sullivan   35
4   Existential-Humanist Bodies of Thought   53
5   Behavioral Approaches.   69
6   Cognitive Approaches to Therapy 89
7   Reality Therapy 101
8   Communications/Interaction Theory. 113
9   Social Ecological Approaches 131
10 Community Mental Health 147
11 Deviance or Labeling Theory 161

1

The Medical Model

Any discussion of the medical model must begin with the qualification that no universally accepted version of the medical model exists.[2] This chapter presents the medical model in its classical and purest form, leaving out proposed extensions, alterations, and reformulations.

The medical model is strictly in the possession of medicine, though aspects of it have been used in other paramedical or allied health disciplines. It is both an ideology and a collection of knowledge, which cannot be effectively separated. The ideological component of the medical model includes a set of beliefs about the physician's role as a healer with authority over patients. The knowledge component is a reductionist, biochemical body of information that explains disease as an interruption of normal physiological processes and yields procedures to eliminate disease through manipulation or alteration of somatic structures and processes. The medical model can thus be defined as the beliefs and knowledge that define physicians as authoritative healers and that enable them to cure, ameliorate, or arrest disease through recognition and alteration of its manifestation in bodily states.

HISTORY AND PURPOSE

The current medical model can be partially traced to the medical systems of the ancient Greeks.[5] Hippocrates is viewed as the progenitor of modern medicine, and while his writings presage the medical model, they reflect a broader viewpoint. The Hippocratic view of medicine is based on the ideas embodied in two Grecian gods.

Hygeia, the goddess of health, represented the concepts that health is a state of harmony with nature and one's environment and that disease results from violation of natural laws that govern this harmony. Hygeia was a teacher of wisdom who represented living in an orderly and harmonious fashion as a protection against the ravages of disease. The god, Asclepius, embodied the healer—one who cures with medicinal plants and surgery. The Asclepian authority of the physician derives from this divine healer.[19] Whereas Hygeia disseminated practical knowledge to the populace to guide their actions, Asclepius wielded esoteric knowledge as part of his healing art. He ministered to a passive and compliant recipient of the healing action. Because he was the knowing healer, his authority over the patient was absolute.

Hippocrates took a democratic view of the relative importance of these two modes of medical practice, stressing the role of the physician as both a teacher and a healer.[5] In that sense, Hippocratic medicine is broader than the current medical model, which exclusively embraces the Asclepian mode. Hippocrates does portend one important element of the medical model, namely, its commitment to science. He called for the liberalization of scientific medicine from theological (i.e., mystical and demonic) beliefs.

The history of Western medicine is one of steady growth of scientific knowledge concerning disease and its management.[5] The powers of observation, analytic thought, and experimentation catapulted medicine into one of the most successful enterprises known to human civilizations. This was made possible by the confinement of medical knowledge to the domain of reductionistic cause-and-effect perspectives and to biological phenomena. That is, medical knowledge is concentrated on underlying biochemical constituents of the human body and their cause-and-effect relationships, with a relative lack of concern for more complex biological phenomena, psychosocial phenomena, and connections between mind and body.

At the time when medicine began to increase its scientific base, reductionist thought in the physical sciences was reaching maturity. Scientists had made great strides in understanding the physical world through careful examination of the building blocks of nature and their interrelationships.[4] They sought to understand the universe as a great clockwork of interacting parts. Both the separation of mind from body and this "mechanistic" viewpoint of reductionist science led medicine to adopt the view of the body as a machine and led physicians to adopt the view that their task was to repair breakdowns in the machine (i.e., disease).[4] In practice, physicians using the medical model came to treat the body as separate from psychological and social processes and tended to see the latter as insignificant.

The most central aspect of the medical model is the concept of disease. Foucault[8] documents the long history of medical thought that culminates in the physician's ability to separate the person who is experiencing an illness from the underlying disease that "resides within" the person. This abstraction is at the core of all medical thought and practice.

Historically, the medical model has been the nearly exclusive domain of physicians; in turn, physicians have largely chosen to approach their practice within the framework of the medical model. Psychiatry, however, represents

4

a rather unusual case. Psychiatry's relationship to mainstream medicine has been and remains a matter of concern among physicians. Some believe that psychiatry is a branch of medicine that has collected a variety of perspectives, knowledge, and skills that extend beyond the traditional purview of medicine. They view this as a necessary response to patients' psychosocial problems. Others disagree, arguing that the medical model alone defines both the physician's role and domain of concern. Proponents of the latter viewpoint would support a narrowing of psychiatric practice to concentrate on those psychosocial problems that are true biological diseases, leaving to other health professionals psychosocial problems that have no biological components.

VIEW OF ORDER

The theory base of the medical model includes three major themes: (1) a reductionist cause-and-effect framework, (2) a concern with the biochemical level of structures and processes, and (3) a homeostatic or normative view of order. These are interrelated in the theoretical explanation of health (order). Because the medical model has traditionally been concerned primarily with disorder, the approach to defining order has been to proceed "inductively by enumeration of examples [of disease] and then health is the absence of all of those states" (p. 75).[3] The problem of what constitutes order in the human system is generally not a major issue in the medical model, simply because the prime focus of concern is disorder.

Reductionism and the cause-and-effect conceptualizations of the medical model are derived from the intellectual models of early physical sciences.[4,17] The basic tenets of reductionism are that any phenomenon is ultimately reducible, and thus explicable, in terms of its most elementary constituents and their cause-and-effect relationships.[1,4] In physical science, reductionist strategies were the searches for the building blocks of the inanimate world. They led to such discoveries as the atom—at one time considered the building block of physical phenomena. In the biological sciences and in medicine, the search led to the discovery of the cell and later its molecular constituents, their chemical components, and so forth. Always, reductionism progresses deeper into the system in the search for more and more elemental parts. The goal of reductionist thought is that ultimately all phenomena at a macro level (e.g., bodily functions directly observable to anyone) will be explained in terms of the finite cause-and-effect relations between the most elementary or microlevel components of the body. Thus, tissue can be understood in terms of its cellular makeup, cells in terms of their molecular structures, molecules in terms of their chemical constituents, and so forth.

As a function of its reductionist strategy, the medical model has less concern for macro events (i.e., the body functioning as a whole, as an instrument of the mind, and as an embodiment of someone who has a social position). Rather, the medical model considers psychosocial factors as either inconsequential or as irrelevant to its domain of concern and concentrates on the underlying biological and chemical level. Thus, order primarily refers to integrity of the biochemical constituents of the body.[2,7]

The medical model has also viewed order as homeostasis, a central concept in medical thinking. The classic concept of homeostasis[1] is the notion that living systems try to maintain certain predetermined states. Any substantial movement from a homeostatic state is disturbance to the order of the system. Examples of homeostatic processes in the body are blood pressure and temperature. When conditions change from what is typical for the organism, it seeks to return them to that previous state. Thus, the concept of order in the medical model refers primarily to the maintenance of those bodily states that are considered to be normal.

VIEW OF DISORDER

In the medical model, disorder is disease. As noted earlier, one of the central features of the emergence of the medical model was the ability of the physician to see a disease *in* the person. Thus, disorder is viewed as a correlate to a foreign and disruptive entity dwelling within someone. As Laing and Esterson[11] describe it:

> When a psychiatrist diagnoses schizophrenia, he means that the patient's experience and behavior are disturbed *because* there is something the matter with the patient that causes the disturbed behavior he observed. He calls this something schizophrenia, and he then must ask what causes schizophrenia. (p. ii)

In addition, disease is viewed as disrupting the homeostatic order of biological processes. Disease forces certain functions out of bounds, beyond normative limits. Thus, disease represents an attack on an otherwise static order within the system.

In the purest sense, the medical model view of psychosocial problems is that "mental disorders are in fact organic diseases" (p. 911).[2] This extreme position does not represent all of current psychiatric thought, but it is most consistent with the medical model views of nonpsychiatric physicians. Further, such a characterization of the medical model differentiates it from more psychological concepts often used by psychiatrists, such as psychoanalytic thought.

In the strict sense, the medical model is an *organic* model of mental illness. Physiological disturbances must be present if psychosocial problems are to be considered true diseases.[14] Importantly, for the medical model to yield typical medical treatment, there must be physiological dimensions, if not causes, of the psychosocial disorder. True diseases must have a biological component, as is clear from the following assessment of the medical model view of disorder:

> The dominant model of disease today is biomedical, with molecular biology its basic scientific discipline. It assumes disease to be fully accounted for by deviations from the norm of measurable biological (somatic) variables. It leaves no room within its framework for the social, psychological, and behavioral dimensions of illness. The biomedical model not only requires that disease be dealt with as an entity independent of social behavior, it also demands that behavioral aberrations be explained on the basis of disordered somatic (biochemical or neurophysiological) processes. Thus, the biomedical model embraces both reductionism, the philosophic view that complex phenomena are ultimately derived from a single primary principle, and mind-body dualism, the doctrine that separates the mental from the somatic. (p. 130)[6]

While this view is not accepted by all physicians, those of opposing viewpoints might be said to be operating outside the medical model in their practice and thought. Therefore, biological disturbance *must* accompany psychosocial problems in order to confer upon them disease status.[2,14] Further, problems without any clear organic correlates are problems with living, which fall outside the domain of medicine.[19] This is a somewhat controversial position, but it is most closely in line with traditional concepts of the medical model.

Biological factors, however, need not be the sole cause or manifestation of psychiatric diseases. Although this allows that other causes of psychosocial disorder (e.g., environmental or experiential factors) may well exist and probably do contribute to many psychiatric problems, the medical model seeks to explain *only* the biological components or causes of psychosocial problems.[14]

The medical model categorizes psychiatric diseases as neuropsychiatric, medicopsychiatric, and functional psychiatric.[14] Neuropsychiatric diseases emanate from nervous system disorders (e.g., epilepsy or brain tumor) and medicopsychiatric from other medical conditions (e.g., vitamin deficiency). The functional category refers to problems where organic factors are suspected but not yet proven. Excluded from any of these categories are problems with living, such as situational depressions, social deviances, and adjustment reactions. This particular system of classification differs from the *Diagnostic and Statistical Manual of Mental Disorders III* of the American Psychiatric Association, which avows no particular theoretical leanings, and is not offered as a medical model approach to psychiatric illness. It draws in eclectic fashion from the perspectives of many health disciplines, including occupational therapy. There is obviously a difference between the practical and often multifaceted collections of perspectives used by psychiatrists and the pure medical model.

ACTION IMPLICATIONS

Strictly speaking, action which is derived from the medical model is somatic in nature and guided by the germ theory of disease. According to germ theory, disease has an identifiable cause. Control of disease is best accomplished by attacking the causative agent or focusing treatment on that part of the body affected by disease.[5] The primary emphasis is on discovery of a drug or procedure that would attack the disease or alter or excise the diseased component. This requires that the physician begin with careful data to arrive at a correct diagnosis—the diagnosis is the crux of medical treatment. The following passage aptly describes the action process of the medical model:

> The view of medical practice in effect at the beginning of this century—which we may label the "traditional view"—assumed the existence of a set of discrete entities called diseases and a set of other entities called therapies or therapeutic agents. These two sets were thought to be related in an imperfect 1:1 correspondence. The task of the physician was to classify signs and symptoms to determine which of the disease entities were present in his patient. When successful, this process of diagnosis suggested the corresponding therapy which the physician was to apply. (p. 83)[3]

Identifying the disease ordinarily means that the physician will have some degree of ability to predict and control the course of illness. The diagnosis is critical in the medical model, because it predicts the course of treatment and the path of the disease.[15] If treatment is successful, it then confirms the physician's initial diagnosis.

However, only in the case of a limited number of diseases does medicine reach this ideal of sufficient knowledge in order to make efficacious use of the diagnosis.[15] There is a continuum from those diseases for which there is rather certain knowledge of etiology, course, and treatment, to those about which little or nothing is known. Psychosocial problems fall at the latter end of the continuum.

The primary somatic therapies of the medical model are chemotherapy, electroconvulsive therapy, diet management, and surgery.[14] A variety of chemotherapies are used for psychosocial disturbances, or to control or manage other biological problems that are concomitants of the psychosocial problem (e.g., the control of epilepsy). The major use of drugs in psychosocial practice is for the management of psychiatric symptomatology. These psychotropic drugs may be divided into antipsychotics, antidepressants, and minor tranquilizers.[10]

Antipsychotics include several families of related chemical compounds. They are used to reduce the extreme symptomatology of psychotic patients. These drugs routinely have a variety of side effects ranging from the fairly innocuous, such as a dry mouth, to serious and some possibly irreversible complications, such as seizure and tardive dyskinesia.

Antidepressant drugs also include several families of chemicals. These drugs palliate symptoms of clinical depression with fewer side effects than the antipsychotic drugs. Minor tranquilizers are a family of drugs generally used to alleviate the symptom of anxiety, and they are more often given to non-hospitalized patients.[10] Their major side effect is sedation.

In all cases, the drugs, within their major categorizations, may act variously with different patients. Optimal dosage is also a matter of great variation among patients. Thus, medication with psychotropic drugs ordinarily involves a trial-and-error period during which both the desired results and side effects are monitored in order to achieve correct prescription. However, since the variety of antipsychotics is great but effects are generally similar, the choice of drugs is largely based on physician familiarity and preference.

Psychosurgery for psychiatric symptoms (e.g., the classic lobotomy) is much less frequent today. The most likely situation for surgery is removal of an actual brain defect such as a tumor or correction of a somatic problem such as epilepsy. Other somatic therapies such as electroconvulsive therapy and megavitamin therapy tend to vary in their use with the particular clinical conviction of the physician and with diagnoses. Certain psychosocial problems (e.g., mental retardation from phenylketonuria) have been successfully prevented through somatic therapy.

Often, treatment cannot be directed at underlying causes (which may not be known) and instead focuses on managing problems concurrent with the psychosocial disturbance or with managing symptoms without affecting the underlying problem.[14] This means that medical model treatment may be curative, compensatory, syndromatic, or symptomatic.[15] In curative treatment, causative agents are attacked and the condition is reversed. Compensatory treatment aims to minimize further problems and maintain function, while syndromatic treatment manages major problems related to the disease without cure. Finally, symptomatic treatment simply alleviates some problems without altering basic causes or effects of the disease. Only a very small percent of medical treatment is curative.[14]

An interesting aspect of psychiatrists' practice is that while they employ elements of the medical model (e.g., Asclepian authority and diagnostic procedures), treatment often includes a variety of approaches (e.g., behavior modification and psychotherapy) informed by bodies of knowledge other than the medical model. These are loosely viewed as compatible with the medical model.[14]

CRITICISMS AND LIMITATIONS

Engel[6,7] argues that the medical model leaves only two alternatives for reconciling the relationship between disease and behavior: (1) a reductionistic alternative, which is to say that all odd or disordered behavior results from or is caused by disease; and (2) an exclusionistic alternative, which says that behavioral disorders that cannot be explained in biochemical terms must be excluded from the category of disease. Engel also argues that the reductionism of the medical model has led to undesirable treatment practices such as overuse of surgery and drugs and inappropriate use of diagnostic procedures. He criticizes the medical model for its lack of concern for factors other than the biomedical.

The value of diagnostic procedures is directly related to the certainty of etiological and therapeutic implications of the diagnosis. This requires that much be known about the disease, its course, its alterability, and the agents that have power to control the disease processes. Many persons have criticized the use of psychiatric diagnostic processes in the medical model, because in psychiatry few diagnoses approach the degree of knowledge and certainty needed for effective delineation of etiology, course (prognosis), and treatment. Goffman[9] notes in this vein that:

> While some psychiatric cases may be neatly handled within the framework established by the medical model there are very evident sources of difficulty, especially in regard to the largest category of patients, those with so-called "functional" psychoses. (p. 352)

Others argue that it will never be correct to apply diagnostic procedures to psychiatric medicine because psychosocial problems are not diseases but rather problems with living.[13,20]

Recognizing that mental illness appears to involve a complex of social factors, psychological factors, biological factors, and their interrelationships points to the need for a model that can address multilevel, complex phenomena. Matching one-to-one therapies for given psychosocial problems with a mechanistic disease-therapy model is simply not possible.[13]

Leifer[13] has launched one of the most critical attacks on the medical model, claiming that it is an ideological rather than a therapeutic tool in the hands of psychiatry. He compares similarities and differences between psychiatry and somatic medicine, noting that the similarities lie more in the background and the conceptual and ideological views held by physicians than in their patients. Criticizing the purely medical model approach to mental disease, he notes that the "important distinction between medical and mental disease is that action to eliminate the former is directed against bodies while action to eliminate the latter is directed against persons" (p.16).[13] Leifer further notes that it is important "whether psychiatric patients are viewed as suffering from diseases or as experiencing some other kinds of problems" (p. 13).[13] He insists that disease should refer to phenomena not regulated by social customs and belonging to organic structure and function of the body. By calling mental illness a disease, the medical model obscures the fact that psychiatrists are agents of social control. Thus, he concludes, while the work of other physicians is primarily a technical matter, the work of psychiatry is patently moral and political in nature. Leifer[13] concludes that conceptual models are metaphors and they reveal only what is congenial to their form, disguising or diverting attention from those things they cannot assimilate. He calls for an expanded biosocial model of mental illness, identifies the need to conduct research into the relationship between the mind and body, and feels that the medical model in psychiatry impedes this process.

Similarly, Szasz sees the medical model as a sham that obscures psychiatry's real role and justifies wholesale segregation and incarceration of socially deviant individuals.[20] Szasz distinguishes between diseases of the body and what he calls "problems with living." The former are properly the purview of medicine while the latter are in the field of human relations and thus constitute a moral rather than a scientific enterprise.

Laing and Esterson emphatically take issue with the assertion that schizophrenia is an entity, clinical or otherwise. They fundamentally disagree with the medical conceptualization of schizophrenia that asserts that "the patient's experience and behavior are disturbed *because* there is something the matter with the patient that causes the disturbed behavior" (p. 11).[11] They criticize the attempt to use the medical model in psychiatry, claiming that it merely represents an attempt to bring psychiatry in line with mainstream biochemical medicine. Attempts to categorize the behavior and experience of persons with psychosocial dysfunction as symptoms are also seen as artificial strategies for making psychiatric practice more medical. Their alternate proposal is that the social intelligibility of schizophrenic thinking and behavior can be understood by examining the family context of the person identified as schizophrenic.

These major criticisms of the medical model pertain to its limited scope (i.e., biochemical, cause-and-effect concepts) and its irrelevance to many psychosocial problems which likely have their etiology and manifestation at the psychological and social levels. Further, there is disagreement with the approach of diagnosing psychosocial patients, both because most psychiatric diagnoses give only limited information about etiology, prognosis, and treatment, and because they presume the existence of biological disease—a phenomenon discounted by some critics.

In sum, the medical model is relevant to psychosocial dysfunction when psychosocial problems have biological concomitants. Chemotherapy is typically of some use in the management of symptoms. In a few categories of psychosocial problems, physicians can have direct impact on underlying causes. Thus, the medical model has a contribution to make, but not one that warrants the predominance of physician authority in the area of psychosocial dysfunction.

COMMENTARY

Earliest occupational therapy (see the discussion of moral treatment, Chapter 12) was an attempt to deal outside the medical model with psychiatric patients. Rogers[18] points out cogently that there are critical differences between occupational therapy's approach to order and disorder and that of the medical model. So called "problems with living" and those psychosocial aspects of mental disability eschewed by the medical model are the primary concern of occupational therapy. Further, occupational therapy seeks primarily to influence health rather than pathology.[16] In that sense, the respective contributions of the medical model and occupational therapy would be complementary in the area of psychosocial problems, if occupational therapy is granted authority for the management of problems that fall primarily in its domain.

Unfortunately, the Asclepian authority of medicine extends beyond the domain of the medical model into areas where other health practitioners might better serve as primary caregivers or managers of psychosocial services. An apt guideline offered by Siegler and Osmond[19] is that the physician's role does not include states of impairment. Psychosocial dysfunction often entails major impairment of function which must be regained through substantial rehabilitative efforts. Occupational therapists should be aware of both the strengths and limitations of the medical model and of the particular ways in which occupational therapy can make primary contributions to the care of those with psychosocial problems.

SUMMARY

History and Purpose	The medical model is both knowledge and ideology which defines and justifies the physician's role as an Asclepian authority.
	It emerges from a commitment to science as practiced by the physical sciences and focuses on the process of identifying and eradicating diseases that dwell within persons.

View of Order	Concern is with cause-and-effect relations in biochemical structures and processes.
	Order is equated with homeostatic or normative states and defined primarily as the absence of disorder.
	Because medicine employs reductionist science, which delves deeper and deeper into the organism, its concern with order is micro (biochemical) rather than macro (the person functioning as a whole).
View of Disorder	Disorder is disease, which is viewed as a foreign entity dwelling in the human body and causing a disturbance of the homeostasis or normative order.
	Disorder is viewed in biochemical terms. Psychosocial problems without biochemical constituents or causes are, strictly speaking, not included in the medical model view of disorder.
Action Implications	Medical treatment is somatic and guided by the germ theory of disease which entails identifying causes and eradicating disease and/or its symptoms through: chemotherapy, diet therapy, electroconvulsive therapy, and surgery.
Criticisms and Limitations	Critics fault the medical model for using Asclepian authority for social control of deviance when the nature of psychosocial problems does not warrant a medical model approach.
	The medical model is also criticized for being too reductionist and narrow in its view of disorder.
	The relevance of the medical model is limited to psychosocial problems with biochemical correlates and causes.
Commentary	Occupational therapy and the medical model can offer complementary action when the authority of the latter is limited to areas of relevance and when occupational therapy's relevance to "problems with living" is acknowledged.

TERMS AND CONCEPTS

antidepressants	drugs used to alleviate depression.
antipsychotics	drugs used to alleviate psychotic symptoms.
Asclepian authority	a term used to refer to the physician's right to be the ultimate authority in medicine and to expect compliance. It connotes the idea of a moral right to authority.
chemotherapy	the use of drugs to manage disease and/or its symptoms.
compensatory treatment	treatment aimed at minimizing further problems and maintaining function.
curative treatment	treatment aimed at attacking the causative agent and reversing the condition.
electroconvulsive therapy	the use of electric shock to alleviate symptoms of certain mental disorders.
epilepsy	a disorder in which those afflicted experience seizures.
etiology	the source or cause of a disease or dysfunction.
homeostatic	a process of maintaining a static state and returning to it after disturbances (examples are rate of heartbeat and blood pressure).
lobotomy	removal of a portion of the brain usually to reduce aggressive behavior.
medicopsychiatric disease	disease emanating from biochemical disturbances other than those in the nervous system.
minor tranquilizers	drugs used to reduce anxiety.
neuropsychiatric disease	disease emanating from disorders in the nervous system.
problems with living	a phrase used to refer to psychosocial problems which appear to have no biological cause, but reflect difficulty adjusting to life situations and life tasks.
psychosurgery	surgery that involves removal of brain tissue or implantation of devices to affect electrochemical functions in the brain.

reductionist　　　　　　　a viewpoint that focuses on the components of phenomena and their cause-and-effect relationships, assuming that the whole can be explained through description of how its parts intermesh.

symptomatic treatment　　treatment that alleviates symptoms or problems, but not the underlying disorder or disease.

REFERENCES

1. von Bertalanffy, L. General systems theory and psychiatry. In S.R. Arieti (ed.), *American handbook of psychiatry* (Vol. 3). New York: Basic Books, 1966.
2. Blaney, P. H. Implications of the medical model and its alternatives. *American Journal of Psychiatry*, 1975, *132*, 911–914.
3. Brody, H. The systems view of man: Implications for medicine, science, and ethics. *Perspectives in Biology and Medicine*, 1973, Autumn, 71–92.
4. Capra, F. *The turning point: Science, society, and the rising culture.* New York: Simon & Schuster, 1982.
5. Dubos, R. *The mirage of health.* New York: Harper & Row, 1959.
6. Engel, G. L. The nature of disease and the care of the patient: The challenge of humanism and science in medicine. *Rhode Island Medical Journal*, 1962, *65*, 245–251.
7. Engel, G. L. The need for a new medical model: A challenge for bio-medicine. *Science*, 1977, *196*, 129–135.
8. Foucault, M. [*The birth of the clinic*] (A. M. S. Smith, trans.). New York: Pantheon Books, 1973.
9. Goffman, E. *Asylums.* New York: Doubleday, 1962.
10. Kline, N., & Davis, J. M. Psychotropic drugs. *American Journal of Nursing*, 1973, *73*, 54–62.
11. Laing, T. D., & Esterson, A. *Sanity, madness and the family.* Baltimore: Penguin Books, 1970.
12. Lazare, A. Hidden conceptual models in clinical psychiatry. *New England Journal of Medicine*, 1973, *288*, 345–350.
13. Leifer, R. Medical model as ideology. *International Journal of Psychiatry*, 1970, *9*, 13–34.
14. Ludwig, A. M., & Othmer, E. The medical basis of psychiatry. *American Journal of Psychiatry*, 1977, *134*, 1087–1092.
15. Mechanic, D. The doctor's view of disease and the patient. In D. Mechanic (ed.), *Medical sociology* (2nd ed.). New York: Free Press, 1978.
16. Reilly, M. Occupational therapy can be one of the great ideas of 20th

century medicine. *American Journal of Occupational Therapy*, 1962, *16*, 1–9.

17. Riley, J. N. Western medicine's attempt to become more scientific: Examples from the United States and Thailand. *Social Science and Medicine*, 1977, *11*, 549–560.

18. Rogers, J. Order and disorder in medicine and occupational therapy. *American Journal of Occupational Therapy*, 1982, *36*, 29–35.

19. Siegler, M., & Osmond, H. *Models of madness, models of medicine*. New York: Harper & Row, 1974.

20. Szasz, T. *The myth of mental illness*. New York: Delta, 1961.

2

Classical Psychoanalysis

Psychoanalysis was one of the first systematic approaches to understanding and treating mental illness. A distinguishable approach to the treatment of mental illness as early as 1895, it has become identified and merged with the entire domain of general psychology.[3] For the layman as well as for those professionals who are psychoanalytically oriented, classical psychoanalysis is nearly synonymous with the name of Sigmund Freud, who initiated and developed it.

Psychoanalysis underwent significant changes throughout Freud's 40-year period of active theorizing and practice. While many subsequent psychoanalysts have interpreted and extended his writings, this presentation of classical psychoanalysis will include only the original theories of Sigmund Freud and significant elaborations and interpretations that are congruent with Freud's basic theory. Neo-Freudian theories, which tend to dispute major tenets of Freudian thinking, are presented in the next chapter.

HISTORY AND PURPOSE

The development of psychoanalysis was influenced by then current scientific and social trends and reflects Freud's personal and career development, his medical training, and his professional influences. Several notable scientific and social influences and special interests pervade Freud's work.

The Helmholtz school of physiology that emphasized cause and effect sequential thinking and the belief that all science could be reduced to the laws of physics had a strong impact on Freud's works.[1] Freud believed that explaining human psychological functioning in terms of scientific laws was not only possible, but offered the best means of clearly understanding human behavior. The following quote characterizes his views on this issue:

The hypothesis we have adopted of a psychical apparatus extended in space, expediently put together, developed by the exigencies of life, which gives rise to the phenomena of consciousness only at one particular point and under certain conditions—this hypothesis has put us in a position to establish psychology on foundations similar to those of any other science, such, for instance, as physics . . . . Our procedure in psycho-analysis is quite similar. We have discovered technical methods of filling up the gaps in the phenomena of our consciousness, and we make use of those methods just as a physicist makes use of experiment. In this manner we infer a number of processes which are themselves "unknowable" and interpolate them in those that are conscious to us. (pp. 53-54)[6]

Other influences reflected in Freud's work include a personal interest in Shakespeare and Goethe, Victorian English values (especially those relative to sexuality), and the flourishing, yet controversial Darwinian theory of evolution.[1,5] Thus, while his theories were original, they reflected both sophisticated intellectual trends of his day as well as other social and cultural influences.

Freud was born in 1856 in an area now called Czechoslovakia. When he was 4, Freud's family moved to Vienna, where he eventually received a medical degree and centered his life and career. In the 1920s he fled from Nazism to England, where he died in 1939.[1,5]

Before settling on the study of psychological phenomena, Freud had a varied medical background. He originally worked as a neurological and neuroanatomical researcher. Then in private practice he worked as a general physician, surgeon, and finally as a psychiatrist at the Vienna General Hospital under Theodor Meynert, a leading brain anatomist. Later, Freud studied at the neurology clinic of Jean-Martin Charcot in Paris, where he developed an interest in hysteria and in the use of hypnosis as a psychiatric treatment. Although Freud eventually found hypnosis to be a limited treatment technique, his interest in it led to more concern with inner, unconscious phenomena. Freud then worked with the Viennese physician Josef Breuer to begin development of what he called a "talking out" technique that is still the primary method of psychoanalysis.[2,5] It is at this point, during Freud's work with Breuer in the study of hysteria and the use of hypnosis, that psychoanalysis has its identifiable origins.

Freud's development of psychoanalytic theories has been identified as reflecting six stages.[1] The first was the period of collaboration with Breuer. Together they described hysterical symptoms as being caused by pent-up emotion related to an unpleasant event stored in the unconscious. Treatment involved helping the patient to recall the memory of this event from the unconscious and express the related emotion, effecting relief and release of undischarged energy. This process was termed "cathartic abreaction." Freud noted that such traumatic events often occurred in childhood and were routinely sexual in nature. This led to his theorizing about childhood sexuality.[1] Freud eventually split with

Breuer over the former's sexual emphasis, and he was ostracized from one of the prominent medical societies for the same reason.

The second stage, around 1900, began with the study of dreams. Freud noted that dreams and symptoms bore strong similarities; both seemed to be distortions formed by the tension between the forces of unconscious childhood wishes seeking expression and the other aspects of mental life exerting a controlling or repressive effect on these wishes. Freud's insights and understandings came about partly from self-analysis. His most significant thesis was that mental life is primarily characterized by dynamics of conflict between the conscious and unconscious—that is, between what is realistic and logical versus sexual and impulsive. This theory is called the *topographic theory* since it relates to layers of consciousness.[1]

In the third stage, Freud sought an explanation for psychotic behavior. The tension between sexual urges and the more adaptive, logical mental forces seemed inadequate for explaining psychoses. He theorized that tension between investing libidinal energies (sexual drives) in the self versus objects external to the self better explained psychotic behavior.[1] The fourth stage was his attempt at synthesis and reorganization; he tried to organize his concepts as a metapsychology. This was a transitional phase prior to a major theory revision.[1] In the next stage, Freud revised his drive theory to make it a dualistic theory including both libido (sex) and aggression, which are derived respectively from broader biological bases called Eros (love) and Thanatos (the death instinct).[1]

In the sixth and final stage, Freud formed his *structural theory* of the mind's organization, in which the components of mental function were identified by the roles they played in conflict. He divided the psychic apparatus into id, ego, and superego. Mental health and mental illness were viewed as dependent on how well the ego mediated between mental conflicts and external reality factors. Anxiety was identified as a warning signal of mental imbalance, alerting the ego to activate a defensive strategy for self-protection.[1]

The current status of psychoanalysis in the United States is largely influenced by policies of the psychoanalytic training institutes affiliated with the American Psychoanalytic Association. With a few exceptions, they limit their admissions to those with a medical degree who have completed a psychiatric training residency. Thus, in-depth psychoanalysis in this country is provided mainly by psychiatrists. However, other mental health disciplines receive training from psychoanalytic organizations not restricted to medical doctors and frequently provide care based on psychoanalytic concepts.[1]

VIEW OF ORDER

Describing the view of order in psychoanalytic theory seems paradoxical since psychoanalytic concepts were developed by Freud largely in response to and from observation of pathological processes. However, some themes that characterize how the human being's mental processes interrelate and unfold can be said to constitute a view of order—though, in the end, psychoanalysis gives the clear impression that order is less probable than disorder in the human being.

The view of order in psychoanalytic thinking reflects linear cause-and-effect thinking, concern with levels of consciousness, the views that causation always comes from lower, more covert levels and that human actions always seek to avoid tension or disequilibrium.

Order is a function of drives that emanate from biological inheritances. These drives are mediated and interrelated at different levels of consciousness though they emanate from lower levels. Conflict is a pivotal feature of all mental processes, and order involves the process of minimizing conflict or tension. Psychoanalysis is a "psychology of conflict" (p. 1),[1] and much as behaviorists consider a person's outward behavior to result from attempts at tension-reduction, psychoanalysts see the operation of the mind to be a product of attempts to reduce or adjust to tensions within the psychic apparatus. These tensions exist between the conscious and the unconscious, internal and external demands, and also result from demands on the organism for growth and development. Many of the themes and principles of psychoanalysis reflect this concern with conflict.

Psychoanalytic Principles

Four major principles of psychoanalytic theory are psychic determinism, the topographic viewpoint, the dynamic viewpoint, and the genetic viewpoint.[1]

Psychic determinism argues that mental events such as feelings and thoughts have specific causes; these are often unconscious and related to earlier life events.

According to the *topographic viewpoint*, mental events are organized into layers of consciousness—the conscious, preconscious, and unconscious. The conscious level is the same consciousness referred to in daily conversation. That content which is easily remembered describes the preconscious. Other psychic material that is inaccessible to the conscious and must be inferred or otherwise recognized is in the unconscious. Conflicts arise from efforts to move psychic material from one level to another or to keep it on one particular level of awareness. A dynamic related to the topographic viewpoint is repression, the process of keeping mental material from conscious awareness to avoid unpleasant events. Another dynamic, resistance, occurs in the analysis when the ego of the patient persistently opposes the perceived threat of the analysis process and the moving of unconscious content to levels of greater awareness.[6] Overcoming this resistance is a significant part of the analyst's work. This topographic theory has been supplanted by Freud's structural theory (i.e., his reference to the id, ego, and superego) as a more useful guide to practice.

The third principle of psychoanalytic theory is the *dynamic viewpoint*. This refers to forces that interact, stimulating the mind to function and change. These forces are libidinal and aggressive drives that emanate from the human biological endowment. Freud referred to these drives as ultimate causes of all human activity. Drives—sometimes called need or tension states—function to motivate the organism to act with the goal of tension reduction; action so motivated or caused brings a sense of relief, gratification, or pleasure.[1]

According to Freud these drives were derived from two basic instincts, Eros (love) and Thanatos (the destructive instinct): "The aim of the first of these basic instincts is to establish ever greater unities and to preserve them thus—in short, to bind together; the aim of the second is, on the contrary, to undo connections and so to destroy things" (p. 5).[6] He described their nature as oppositional, resulting in a process of attraction and repulsion. The psychic energy correlate of Eros is the libido, and the correlate of Thanatos is aggression.

The fourth principle of psychoanalytic theory, referred to as the *genetic viewpoint*, traces "origins of later conflicts, character traits, neurotic symptoms, and psychological structure to the crucial events and wishes of childhood and the fantasies they generated" (p. 12).[1] Freud argued for the pivotal role of childhood development in later personality structure. This theme is seen in the development of object relations (i.e., the emotional connections to persons or things, as opposed to one's self-regard). Freud theorized that the selection of love objects in adulthood as well as other object relations revealed in other interests and activities were dependent on the quality and type of object relationships in early childhood. Thus, childhood development has pervasive effects on all later life.

The stages of psychosexual development and the child's discovery of erotogenic zones (body areas that are sensitive and provide a sense of pleasure) is also understood in terms of the genetic viewpoint. According to Freud, erotogenic zones vary as development progresses. Each is tied to psychological development so that faulty psychological development will be evident by the inappropriate predominance in later life of one of these erotogenic zones. The first zone of importance developmentally is the mouth. This is particularly important as a source of nourishment and satisfaction for the infant. Next the anal zone gains importance, as the growing child learns to control excretory functions. The phallic phase follows. During this phase, Freud described different developmental events for boys and girls as they each work out their relationships to the same- and opposite-sexed parents and resolve the related tensions of jealousy and rivalry. Finally, during the genital phase of puberty, no new erogenous areas are discovered, but the events of previous stages are synthesized, and the child begins to direct his or her attention to the opposite sex.[2,6]

Additional Concepts

In Freud's later *structural theory* of the psychic apparatus, he described the psyche as organized into the id, the ego, and the superego. The id exists as a disorganized collection of instinctual drives and related energy; it is genetically inherited. The ego is a collection of functions characterized by concern with self-preservation through avoiding pain while seeking pleasure. Anxiety is the signal to the ego of impending displeasure and alerts the ego to action. The ego serves as mediator between the id's desires and the superego's demands and reality factors. The superego is the mental structure that functions as the moral agent. It is influenced by parental training and contains ideals for action.[5,6]

Anna Freud elaborated on her father's thinking about defense mechanisms. These mechanisms are evident in everyday life as the ego performs its mediating role. While defenses are part of order, they can be pathological if immature mechanisms from pregenital phases of development are used excessively in adulthood. An example of an immature defense is regression, in which a person returns to a developmentally earlier level of function for the purpose of avoiding discomfort in the present. A mature defense may be the use of humor, in which a person expresses feelings without discomfort to self or others.[5]

Order, as suggested by these concepts, is directly related to the adequacy of ego function in protecting the mind from an upsurge of conflictual material through skillful use of defense mechanisms. The difference between mental health and illness relates to how well the ego manages this task. Order is a delicate balance of forces, easily disrupted, or as one author states, it is a "tenuously stable equilibrium" between id, superego, and reality maintained by "successful repression" (p. 16).[1] Order is manifest as "the capacity to need others, to love, to want to please, and to become like others" (p. 15).[1]

VIEW OF DISORDER

Disorder occurs when psychic forces are in conflict and out of balance, when the person cannot appropriately release tension through defenses, when serious conflicts prevent the normal progression through psychosexual stages of development, and when libidinal drives are misplaced.

Neuroses

The disorder most commonly dealt with in classical psychoanalysis is neurosis.

Neurosis results when a balance (order) between the id, superego, and reality is not maintained. Anxiety, a common symptom of neurosis, acts as a warning signal, enabling the ego to mobilize defensive mechanisms that assist in coping or in maintaining this balance.

Freud noted that neurotics experience the same life demands as others and possess the same general dispositions to deal with these demands but suffer greater discomfort and anxiety. Freud's conclusion was that the difference between neurotics and nonneurotics is the ability of some individuals to deal comfortably and effectively with greater demands than others.[6]

Childhood conflicts are seen as playing a central etiological role in the later emergence of neurotic behavior. All children are viewed as having conflicts, and many have neuroses such as apprehensions, nightmares, and phobias. Children's feelings about their parents are seen as a key to understanding their later psychic configuration. The predominant psychoanalytic dogma is that neuroses are acquired in early childhood before the age of six; however, symptoms may not appear until much later. These childhood neuroses seem to pass, yet may reemerge in adulthood when the delicate balance between drives and defenses is upset.[1,8]

Freud noted that "weakening of the ego" (caused by childhood conflicts) is a precondition to psychopathology and that excessive demands may paralyze the ego's functioning and precipitate a state of disorder (p. 29).[6] Examples of excessive ego demands are the overchallenges presented by new developmental tasks (job, role change, etc.), illness, loss, or disappointment. Any of these could create imbalance in a vulnerable psyche and cause anxiety as old childhood conflicts reemerge and the individual turns to immature responses.

Schizophrenia

Freud's original view of the etiology of schizophrenia was that the libido is withdrawn from external objects and invested in the self.[5] This view is personified by the individual who is withdrawn and preoccupied with delusions, hallucinations, and other idiosyncratic thoughts and sensations.

ACTION IMPLICATIONS

Psychoanalysis as a treatment method developed by Freud and his followers will be discussed in terms of the general therapy process, specific therapeutic techniques, the therapist's and patient's roles, the dynamics of therapy, and the desired outcomes of therapy.

In the general *process of psychoanalysis*, the therapist tries to bring repressed mental content back to conscious awareness for the purpose of helping patients recognize their emotional needs, identify unconscious motivation, and find realistic ways to resolve unconscious conflicts. Therapy directly flows from the psychoanalytic view of neurotic disorder, in that treatment aims at curing the basic neuroses, and practitioners pride themselves in this effort, rather than attempting more superficial symptomatic relief. This requires recalling childhood events and reexperiencing, in the context of the therapeutic encounter, one's immature responses, and finally analyzing these responses and one's resistance to treatment.[5]

The *analytic situation* refers to the patient/therapist relationship that provides the necessary context in which therapy can occur. It literally includes certain patient positioning, such as lying on a couch with the therapist unseen, and setting the expectation that the patient be as honest in reporting mental content as possible. It also involves the therapist's maintaining an "attitude of benign curiosity" (p. 19).[1] This situation creates a relationship in which the patient can freely express mental content with as little influence as possible from other forces and in which the therapeutic regression occurs.

The *analytic process* involves the actual therapy phases and the process of the patient's regression. This process can be divided into phases of initiation and establishment of the analytic situation, transference and its analysis, and termination.[5]

In the first phase, everything patients do and say and the ways they act are observed. The nature of the problem is explored in the interview, while the therapist looks for emerging themes in the patient's content and manner of expression. In the second phase, the patient develops an emotional bond with the therapist and begins to relate to the therapist as though the therapist were another significant person in the patient's life. This relationship, called transference, is analyzed, and understanding of the transference relationship is constantly deepened. In the termination phase, the therapeutic relationship is typically ended with the patient temporarily resuming immature behavior in an effort to prolong the relationship. The therapy process can take several years to complete, with therapy sessions as frequent as four times weekly.

Techniques include the use of free association, analysis of the transference relationship, analysis of resistance, and interpretation. *Free association* involves making the unconscious conscious by having the patient report all thoughts, uncensored and regardless of their seeming insignificance.[5] The information revealed may include content from dreams. *Analysis of the transference relationship* is one of the most integral events of therapy. During this, the therapist helps the patient to distinguish current reality from past events and to align more mature, appropriate responses with the present. *Analysis of the patient's resistance* to therapy also provides further insight into personality configuration and dynamics, such as understanding defenses and resistance. These three sources of information about the patient's mental life provide the raw material from which the therapist attempts *interpretation*. The therapist's comments are carefully timed responses shared when the patient is perceived by the therapist to be ready to personally understand or make use of new viewpoints or links. Freud expressed this in the following way:

> As a rule we put off telling him of a construction or explanation till he himself has so nearly arrived at it that only a single step remains to be taken, though that step is in fact the decisive synthesis. (p. 35)[6]

To do this, the therapist needs to be able to empathize with the patient and to work intuitively, by managing the wealth of information meaningfully on other than a conscious level. The therapist must work introspectively, allowing by silent free association an interpretation to surface, which is then validated by the patient.

In summary, the therapist establishes the analytic situation, remaining relatively passive to allow the free, unhampered expression of thoughts. The therapist focuses thoughts on understanding the transference neurosis, and shares carefully timed responses with the patient. The patient's role is to reveal all, uncensored, to the therapist; to work with dedication, discipline, and earnest effort to solve his or her problems; and to accept the fact that the true nature of these problems is unknowable, thus requiring the assistance of a therapist to recognize them. According to Freud, there is a pact between therapist and patient calling for "complete candour on one side and strict discretion on the other" (p. 31).[6]

The core dynamics of psychoanalytic treatment are *remembering* (i.e., recalling childhood experiences) and *reliving* through the transference relationship with the analyst. Strengthening a weak ego requires self-knowledge. Insight and understanding based on remembering and reliving act to strengthen the ego through providing this self-knowledge. They are thus viewed as the crux of basic personality change in therapy.

The nature of treatment outcomes is not considered to be amenable to measurement by current research techniques. Similarly, symptom alleviation is not considered to be the most important outcome of treatment. The ability to derive happiness from life, to deal with normal life stresses, to relate in satisfying ways with others, and, most importantly, the release of the individual's potential which was previously blocked by neurotic conflicts are typical descriptions of preferred treatment outcomes.[5]

Given the personally and intellectually demanding nature of psychoanalysis, it is considered useful only with relatively high functioning patients. It is generally believed to be most valuable with those who are highly motivated to overcome more infantile manifestations of behavior, are able to think logically, have adequate ego strength to endure short-term frustration and anxiety in the interest of long-term benefits, are flexible, have functional assets such as good school or work performance, and maintain an "honest skepticism" about the success of therapy rather than being overly exuberant (p. 266).[5] Additionally, the following patient characteristics are predictive of successful therapy: discipline, ability to verbally express thoughts and feelings, basic honesty, and ability to test reality. Psychoanalysis is considered best suited to those with the disorders of hysteria, anxiety hysteria, obsessive-compulsive neurosis, and other disorders characterized by anxiety. Freud himself saw psychoanalysis as valuable for those with neurotic disorders and as having little benefit for those with psychotic disorders.

CRITICISMS AND LIMITATIONS

Freud acknowledged limitations of his own approach: "It may be that there are other still undreamt-of possibilities of therapy. But for the moment, we have nothing better at our disposal than the technique of psycho-analysis, and for that reason, in spite of its limitations, it should not be despised" (p. 39).[6]

As Freud anticipated, there have been criticisms and reformulations of both his theory and therapeutic technique. Typical examples of criticisms of the psychoanalytic approach are found in Glasser's[7] writings on reality therapy and are implied in the work of behaviorists. Glasser claims that six of the most basic tenets of psychoanalytic theory are invalid: the belief in mental illness and its classification; the probing of the personal, historical roots of the problem; the encouragement and use of transference in treatment; the belief in understanding and insight to effect personality change; the avoidance of the issues related to moral responsibility for behavior; and the disdain of the teaching role of the therapist. He challenges all six points on the basis that psychoanalytic treatment promotes a view of mental illness and therapy that is illness-focused, promotes irresponsible patient behavior, and is mystical and backward-looking rather than focused on the future and the development of adaptive behavior.[7]

Behaviorally oriented therapists criticize the lack of research evidence for effectiveness of psychoanalytic, insight-oriented approaches. These writers note both that there is a lack of research to support the effectiveness of classical psychoanalysis, and that it is expensive and time consuming.[8]

White[12] and other writers have challenged the psychoanalytic view that all motivation springs from tension reduction, libidinal energy, and conflicts. These critics stress that humans have tension-seeking drives that are focused on productivity, control, creativity, and other behaviors having little or nothing to do with sex. Many other criticisms of Freud's exclusive focus on sexual drives have been levied.

Systems theorists criticize psychoanalysis for its overly mechanistic and homeostatic view of humans and for its failure to acknowledge the processes by which humans grow, change, acquire skills and values, and so forth.[11] Finally, psychoanalysis has been criticized as not being relevant to the majority of persons who experience mental disorders and who are not capable of the insight process and verbal demands or who cannot afford its costly treatment.

The work of psychoanalysis has made an important contribution to the understanding of human behavior and motives and cannot be discounted out of hand despite its very clear limitations, errors, and incompleteness. Chapter 3 (The Neo-Freudians) chronicles many of the new ideas that were generated by the insights and discoveries as well as the limitations and weaknesses of classical psychoanalysis.

COMMENTARY

The psychoanalytic approach has been incorporated into some occupational therapy treatment. This occurred in part because of pressure by psychiatry to make psychoanalysis the sole perspective of all mental health workers. Occupational therapists were told explicitly that their use of occupations to influence health could only be explained by psychoanalysis.[9]

In response, therapists developed methods by which crafts could be used to reveal emotions and symbolic themes and as methods to work out feelings and conflicts, as well as to receive gratification at regressed levels of psychosexual development. However, this approach to occupational therapy has been criticized as both abandoning the field's original mission to use occupations to organize behavior and as selling short the real value of occupation. Thus it has been challenged by therapists for being in opposition to both the development of a unique identity for the profession of occupational therapy and to the original tenets of the field. The use of activities as a means of expressing unconscious material and pent-up emotions directly contradicts the use of activities to challenge and promote adaptive behavior. While this issue is taken up later in the chapter on occupational therapy, it appears that classic psychoanalysis has little in common with occupational therapy.

Reilly[10] suggests that occupational therapists can coexist with those using an analytic approach. She points out that the occupational therapist is concerned with the nonsexual areas of motivation and productivity and as such offers its own unique orientation to the problems of psychosocial dysfunction.

Those who have criticized the wholesale transformation of occupational therapy activities into psychoanalytic tools have suggested that as occupational therapy builds an alternate conceptualization of its use of occupations, some useful ideas from psychoanalysis may be revised and retained.[9] The Fidlers,[4] who originally contributed to the development of psychoanalytic applications of occupational therapy, have proposed one such reconceptualization. They incorporate some ideas from psychoanalysis into a newer framework which acknowledges a much broader and nonsexually focused view of occupations—one which conceptualizes occupation as facilitating the growth, development, and integrity of skills, roles, and a positive sense of self. Their work is exemplary for those who wish to examine this issue further.

SUMMARY

History and Purpose	Psychoanalysis was initiated and developed by Sigmund Freud in the late 19th and early 20th centuries. It was influenced by cause-and-effect sequential thinking and the belief that human psychological functioning could be explained in terms of scientific laws.
	Concepts of infantile sexuality, mental conflict, the topographic theory (consciousness as layered), and the structural theory (id, ego and superego) characterize this approach.
View of Order	The view of order paradoxically developed largely in response to and from observation of pathological processes. Although psychoanalysis emphasizes disordered states, some indications of order can be discerned by looking at the theory of how mental processes develop and interrelate.
	Order is a function of drives that emanate from biological inheritances, which are mediated and interrelated at different levels of consciousness. Order involves the process of reducing conflict.
	For order to exist the ego must protect the mind from an upsurge of conflictual material by use of defense mechanisms. Mental health is related to how well the ego manages this task.

View of Disorder	Disorder occurs when psychic forces are in conflict and out of balance, when the person cannot appropriately release tension through defenses, when serious conflicts prevent the normal progression through psychosexual stages of development, and when libidinal drives are misplaced. The disorder most commonly dealt with in classical psychoanalysis is neurosis.
	Childhood conflicts are believed to be largely responsible for later emergence of neurotic behavior by making the person vulnerable in adulthood to excessive ego demands.
Action Implications	The therapy process involves bringing repressed mental content back to conscious awareness for the purposes of increasing insight into past conflicts and current behavior and to enable the patient to work through conflicts. Thus psychoanalytic treatment is a process whereby the patient is led to talk about feelings, recollections, dreams, and thoughts and to develop a relationship with the therapist who analyzes both the patient's verbal renderings and behavior in the relationship.
	Therapeutic techniques include free association, analysis of transference, analysis of resistance, and interpretation.
	Psychoanalysis is believed to be most useful for those with neurotic disorders rather than with psychotic problems.

Criticisms and Limitations	Psychoanalysis has been criticized for promoting a view of therapy that is illness-focused, promotes irresponsible client behavior, and is mystical and backward-looking.
	It is also criticized for lack of research supporting effectiveness and for being inaccessible to many in need due to time and expense requirements.
	Other authors see the view of motivation as emanating purely from tension as an incomplete view. Critics have argued against Freud's strong emphasis on sexual drives.
	Systems theorists criticize psychoanalysis for its overly mechanistic and homeostatic view of humans.
	It has been criticized as being of little use for individuals incapable of the demands for insight and verbal expression.
Commentary	For a while, psychoanalytic concepts were incorporated into occupational therapy practices. This has been criticized as abandoning the field's original commitment to the use of occupations. Classic psychoanalytic knowledge and occupational therapy have little in common although they can coexist.

TERMS AND CONCEPTS

aggressive instinct	a primary motivating force which tends toward destruction. In interaction with libidinal energies, aggression creates conflict.
analysis of transference	the therapist's continued deepening of the patient's understanding of the transference. During this, the patient comes to distinguish current reality from past events and begins to align more mature, appropriate responses with the present.
analytic process	the actual therapy process, which includes the steps of initiation and establishment of the analytic situation, transference and its analysis, and termination.

analytic situation	the patient/therapist relationship in which the expectation is set for the patient to openly express all mental content and for the therapist to listen without influencing the flow of the patient's thoughts.
anxiety	the general negative feeling of uneasiness, fear, and/or apprehension recognized as a common symptom of neurosis. It acts as a warning signal to the ego of mental imbalance, indicating the need to activate defensive strategies for self-protection.
cathartic abreaction	an early treatment technique for hysteria used by Freud in which the patient was helped to recall unpleasant memories from the unconscious and express the related emotion to effect emotional relief and release of undischarged energy.
conscious	mental content of which one is lucidly aware.
drives	tension states that motivate the organism to act in order to reduce tension. The sources of these drives are the love instinct and the aggressive instinct.
dynamic viewpoint	a principle of psychoanalytic theory that refers to the forces that interact, stimulating the mind to function and change. These forces are libidinal and aggressive drives that emanate from the human biological endowment.
ego	a collection of functions characterized by concern with self-preservation through avoiding pain while seeking pleasure. It serves as mediator between the id and superego demands and reality factors.
erotogenic zones	body areas that are sensitive and provide a sense of pleasure.
free association	the process of making the unconscious conscious by having the patient report all thoughts, uncensored and regardless of their seeming insignificance.
genetic viewpoint	a principle of psychoanalytic theory that places the sources of conflict, character traits, symptoms, and the entire psychological configuration in key childhood events.

31

id	a disorganized collection of instinctual drives and related energy that is genetically inherited.
interpretation	the therapist's understanding of all observed patient behavior and verbalization. These insights are carefully timed, being shared by the therapist at the time when the patient is perceived as being on the brink of understanding them.
libidinal energies	sexual drives. These are a primary source of motivation in Freudian theory and derive from the love instinct (Eros), which tends to bind together. In interaction with the aggressive instinct, libidinal energies create conflict.
neurosis	disorder that results from an imbalance between psychic structures and is characterized by anxiety and the use of immature responses to current situations.
preconscious	mental content that is easily remembered, but which is not foremost in awareness.
psychic determinism	the belief that mental events, such as feelings and thoughts, have specific causes that are often unconscious and related to earlier life events.
repression	the process of keeping mental material from conscious awareness to avoid unpleasant events.
resistance	the process in which the ego of the patient in analysis persistently opposes the perceived threat of the analysis process and the necessary moving of unconscious content to levels of greater awareness.
structural theory	a theory of the mind's organization in which components of mental function (the id, ego, and superego) are identified by the roles they play in conflict.
superego	the mental structure that functions as the moral agent. It is influenced by parental training and contains ideals for action.

topographic theory	a description of mental events as being organized into layers of consciousness—the conscious, preconscious, and unconscious.
transference	the emotional bond between the therapist and patient in which the patient begins to relate to the therapist as though the therapist were another significant person from the patient's life.
unconscious	mental content that is inaccessible to keen awareness and must be inferred or otherwise recognized as being in the unconscious.

REFERENCES

1. Arlow, J. A. Psychoanalysis. In R. Corsini (Ed.), *Current psychotherapies* (2nd ed.). Itasca, Ill.: F. E. Peacock, 1979.
2. Bischof, L. J. *Interpreting personality theory* (2nd ed.). New York: Harper & Row, 1970.
3. Brenner, C. *An elementary textbook of psychoanalysis*. New York: Anchor Books, 1974.
4. Fidler, G., & Fidler, J. Doing and becoming: Purposeful action and self-actualization. *American Journal of Occupational Therapy*, 1978, *32*, 305–310.
5. Freedman, A. M., Kaplan, H. I., & Sadock, B. J. Theories of personality and psychopathology: Freudian schools/Sigmund Freud and classical psychoanalysis. *Modern synopsis of comprehensive textbook of psychiatry* (2nd ed.). Baltimore: Williams & Wilkins, 1976. Pp. 227–270.
6. Freud, S. [*An outline of psychoanalysis*] (J. Strachey, trans., rev. ed.). New York: W. W. Norton & Co., 1969.
7. Glasser, W. *Reality therapy: A new approach to psychiatry*. New York: Harper & Row, Perennial Library, 1975.
8. Kanfer, F. H., & Goldstein, A. P. (Eds.). *Helping people change*. New York: Pergamon Press, 1975.
9. Kielhofner, G., & Burke, J. The evolution of knowledge and practice in occupational therapy: Past, present and future. In G. Kielhofner (Ed.), *Health through occupation: Theory and practice in occupational therapy*. Philadelphia: F. A. Davis, 1983.
10. Reilly, M. Occupational therapy can be one of the great ideas of 20th century medicine. *American Journal of Occupational Therapy*, 1962, *16*, 1–9.
11. von Bertalanffay, L. General system theory and psychiatry. In S. Arieti

(Ed.), *American handbook of psychiatry* (Vol. 3). New York: Basic Books, 1969.

12. White, R. Motivation reconsidered: The concept of competence. In H. Proshansky, W. Ittelson, & L. Rivlin (Eds.), *Environmental psychology*. New York: Holt, Rinehart & Winston, 1970.

3

The Neo-Freudians: Adler, Horney, Fromm, and Sullivan

Some of Freud's successors, although still linked with the analytic tradition, did not accept certain key facets of classic psychoanalysis and thus proposed their own revisions and extensions of psychoanalysis.[4] Despite a lack of unanimity among these neo-Freudians, there are global themes that unite their theories. While neo-Freudian thought today is represented by various therapists, four prominent neo-Freudians—Adler, Horney, Fromm, and Sullivan—have been chosen to illustrate the themes and orientation of neo-Freudian thought.

Probably the most basic of neo-Freudian themes is the emphasis placed on understanding behavior within a cultural and interpersonal context, as opposed to understanding it primarily in terms of the libido and the transformation of infantile oral sexuality into a mature heterogenous sexuality.[6,7] Adler, the first to break with Freud, called his school Individual Psychology. He constructed a unified theory of personality development and dynamics that focuses on the person's attitudes toward self and other persons.[6] Similarly, Horney and Sullivan repudiated the primacy of the libidinal and destructive drives so heavily stressed by Freud,[6] and accentuated interpersonal relations, cultural values, and a drive toward self-actualization as key determinants of human behavior.[4,6] Fromm, also considered to be a member of the dynamic-

Some readers may question why Jung was not included in this chapter. Although a neo-Freudian in the sense that Jung broke with Freud to found his own school, analytic psychotherapy, he is generally not linked with any of the other neo-Freudians. His theories are permeated with religion and philosophy, and in this country, he appears to have had more of an influence on literary and philosophical thinking than on psychotherapeutic practices. With the recent growth of mysticism and religious movements, Jung's ideas have become more popular; however, it seems less likely that occupational therapists will encounter Jungian therapists in their settings than therapists who have been following in the traditions of the theorists included in this chapter.

cultural school along with Horney and Sullivan, did not wholly reject Freud's drive theory. However, he criticized it for not recognizing that drives can also be socially determined and that people, unlike animals, are not obliged to solely follow their instincts.[8] Thus, these neo-Freudians disagreed with Freud over his accentuation of the biologically driven nature of the person and his corresponding deemphasis of the role of society and culture in influencing behavior.

In addition, the neo-Freudians objected to the overly reductionist and mechanistic view of personality suggested by Freud's structural theory of the mind. Whereas Freud proposed the tripartite structure of id, ego, and superego, the neo-Freudians proposed concepts that reflected a more holistic view of personality development.

Neo-Freudians also criticized classical psychoanalysis for its pessimistic view of human potential and the required use of nondirective therapeutic techniques, such as free association. In addition, Horney rejected the devaluation of female sexuality associated with the analytic tradition.[7]

The neo-Freudians were primarily concerned with the neurotic individual. Horney's writings explicitly refer to the "neurotic personality," although she loosely applied the concept of neurosis to all maladaptive behavior, including behaviors that psychiatrists would be more apt to label psychotic.[2] Sullivan had extensive clinical experience with both hospitalized schizophrenics and predominantly neurotic private clients; in his lectures he emphasized the necessity of differentiating which treatment techniques were applicable to specific disorders. Adler's influence has been felt in many arenas, partly because he lectured widely and encouraged implementation of his ideas in varied and nontraditional settings such as mental clinics, schools, and juvenile courts.[2] Fromm's writing is less directed to clinical pathologies than to the problems of living encountered by the contemporary person in an industrial society.

HISTORY AND PURPOSE

Adler, a Viennese physician, joined Freud's psychoanalytic circle in 1902. After several years of close association, theoretical differences began to emerge between the two. Adler, convinced that their ideas were fundamentally different, broke with Freud to found a school of Individual Psychology. His theoretical system was probably one of the earliest phenomenological psychologies, in that it focused attention on the importance of subjective interpretation of events.[2] Adler believed that behavior must be studied from the perspective of the individual; that is, that a person's perceptions and interpretations of events direct future behavior; and that values, attitudes, and interests represent the kinds of thoughts one has about reality.[2] By breaking with Freud, Adler set the stage for dissension by other adherents to psycho-analysis. His influence has pervaded the thinking of most neo-Freudians, as well as existentialists, humanists, and cognitive therapists.[5]

Horney also trained as a psychiatrist and classic psychoanalyst. An excellent clinician, her practice led her to doubt certain clinical and theoretical aspects of the classical psychoanalytic system. She gradually developed her own line of thought, rejecting the notion that behavior is determined by a drive toward sexual fulfillment (i.e., the libidinal drive) and contending instead that culture and interpersonal relationships were the clue to understanding neurosis.

Sullivan, a native American, was influenced by Adolph Meyer's theories of psychosocial behavior (elaborated in the occupational therapy chapter) and the thinking of early American humanists.[4] Sullivan's early clinical work was in hospital settings with schizophrenics. After he moved into private practice, he began to develop his own theoretical system, believed by many to rival Freud's in comprehensiveness.[2,4] Among Sullivan's major contributions are his emphasis on the situational determinants (particularly interpersonal) of behavior, his attempt to understand the phenomena of attention and aware-ness, and his description of the therapist as a "participant-observer" in the therapeutic session.[2]

Fromm's writings anticipate the ideas of existentialism (see Chapter 4), while still drawing freely on the ideas of Freud and other schools of psycho-analysis.[4] Trained as a psychologist, sociologist, and psychoanalyst, he used eclectic ideas to influence students of varied traditions. Fromm did not develop a complete theoretical system, nor did he write specifically about psycho-therapeutic processes. Nevertheless, he is generally associated with the dy-namic-cultural theories of Horney and Sullivan because of his belief that the major issue facing the individual is to achieve a loving and productive rela-tionship with one's fellow beings, and that success or failure in this goal will be largely shaped by one's response to the prevailing culture.[4]

VIEW OF ORDER

These neo-Freudians propose a considerably more optimistic view of the person than found in classical psychoanalytic doctrine. They agree that human behavior is culturally embedded and that both positive and negative personal qualities may be environmentally nurtured.[7] Another commonality is a shared emphasis on the unity of behavior. However, each of the neo-Freudians proposed a different set of terminology and events to explain the development of both ordered and disordered behavior.

Three concepts are central to the Adlerian view of order. First is the belief that all people are born with a capacity for "social interest," or a propensity and desire for cooperation with other persons.[1] Second, Adler emphasized that behavior is goal-directed. Personal goals are neither determined by the environment nor by innate drives, but are chosen by the individual on the basis of a "private logic"—the personal truths, convictions, and fictions (or subjective representations of reality) that the individual lives by.[1] Thus, in contrast to Freud's emphasis on innate, biological drives as motivators of behavior, Adler stresses thinking and planning. The third important concept is that, although individuals have certain genetic endowments and encounter various environmental conditions, their use of or response to these givens is a more important determinant of present and future behavior than either the genetic or the environmental conditions. Thus, he espouses a view of human order that relies on personal responsibility and choice rather than uncontrollable inner and external forces.

In Adler's view, the developing child is subject to influences ranging from constitutional to familial. These influences are met with assumptions and interpretations accumulated by the child through experience. From these interpretations, the child creates his or her own version of reality, one which includes priorities for action and/or inaction. These priorities become recognizable as the individual's "life-style."[1]

The life-style includes a hierarchy of goals and plans which underlie one's actions and enable one to meet new situations. The core of the life-style is a "fictional goal," or a subjective image of what the person would like to be.[5] Adler uses the concept of the life-style to explain what he saw as an underlying tendency toward coherence of an individual's behavior. In other words, the life-style comprises a predominantly non-conscious cognitive plan or organization for coping with life events, without being a rigid or predetermined pattern of behavior.[5] Ultimately, Adler's view of order was one in which the psychologically healthy individual developed an altruistic and flexible interest in others and was capable of replacing false values promoted by society with values representing an honest commitment to life and to humanity.[5]

Horney believed that behavior is largely learned in a sociocultural context and that individuals develop response patterns, building on smaller units until larger organizational sets are formed.[2] She saw the basic determinant of behavior as being a need for security, rising from an anxiety common to all infants: "the feeling a child has of being isolated and helpless in a potentially hostile world" (p. 344).[6] This need for security could lead to either adaptive or maladaptive responses. Horney postulated that people have a central "real" self, which, if given appropriate conditions, would become actualized by the individual.[2] This concept presages the belief of humanistic psychologists in an innate drive toward self-actualization (see Chapter 4).

Horney did not write extensively about normal behavior or psychosocial order. However, her concept of conflict and its personal resolution does imply a view of order. Conflict may exist because of discrepancies between one's "ideal" image of what one should be and one's "actual" self. In this sense, it is an intrapersonal concept. But Horney also believed that intrapersonal conflict reflected cultural ambiguities and inconsistencies about values.[2] For instance, in the United States achievement and getting ahead are highly valued at the same time that brotherhood, democracy, and cooperation are praised by religion, schools, and the government. All people incorporate these cultural inconsistencies and experience conflict as a result. It is not the presence or absence of conflict, then, that characterizes order, but the way in which it is handled. Order, therefore, derives from the ability to reconcile discrepancies between the ideal and actual selves, and between oneself and society, in such a way that the "real" self can become actualized.

Sullivan's view of order is the most comprehensive and introduces many new terms. Like Horney and Adler, Sullivan believed that behavior must be understood within the context of interpersonal relations, and like most analysts, he believed that childhood experiences could induce feelings of either anxiety or security.

According to Sullivan, behavior emerges to satisfy two sets of needs. Biological needs lead to the pursuit of satisfactions, while the need to maintain a state of emotional well-being leads to the pursuit of security and a concomitant feeling of euphoria. Because children experience feelings of security and euphoria for behaving in socially valued ways, they become socialized to the mores of their culture. A child's experiences of security, and the behavior associated with them, become privately labeled as the "good me." Experiences that have led to anxiety become known as the "bad me." If the child is surrounded by people who love and respect him or her, then the "good me" predominates and order exists in the child.[6]

Sullivan believed that interpersonal relationships encompassed the attitudes, fantasies, and daydreams that one has about real people, as well as the visible manifestations of these relationships. He therefore was interested in the development of thought patterns and identified three cognitive models through which people progress. The first mode, called "prototaxic," is one in which children experience random, seemingly unconnected sensations and do not perceive themselves as separate from the environment. In the "parataxic" mode children develop an illogical kind of cause-and-effect reasoning, relating events because of the sequence of their occurrence rather than because of logic or reason. The highest mode, "syntaxic," is characterized by the logical and rational use of publicly accepted symbols.[7]

As children mature, different needs emerge, determining what will and will not receive their attention. Children who are not overly anxious learn to fill these needs successfully, become capable of self-respect and respect for others, and develop the inner freedom and resources that will allow them to question or adapt to the current social structure and values.[8]

Fromm's picture of the development of order emphasizes coming to terms with humanity's existential and historical dichotomies. The existential dichotomies facing people are the knowledge of death while we live and the awareness that we will not be able to realize our potentials in our life span. Historical dichotomies refer to contradictions that have been created by society, but to which solutions could be found.[3] An example of a historical dichotomy is the equal potential for good and harm to result from the development of superior technical knowledge and skills, such as nuclear science. Historical contradictions can be rationalized or explained away, denied or ignored, or annulled and canceled through one's actions; existential dichotomies can be buried or faced.[3] Accepting responsibility for one's part in annulling historical dichotomies and facing the truth about existence leads to the realization that meaning in life can only be found through one's own choices and actions.[3] For Fromm, order in life is thus conferred through productive living. Productivity, embodied by an attitude of relatedness to all forms of human activity and by the individual's sense of being in control of his or her abilities, is the only way in which meaning can be created in life.[3] Interestingly, Fromm rejected fewer of Freud's concepts than Adler, Horney, or Sullivan; however, he believed that the essence of human conflict derived not from the biologically driven nature of the person, but from the necessity for each person to find his or her own solution to the historical and existential contradictions of life.[6] The historical and existential dynamic is Fromm's major contribution to understanding human order.

A synthesis of these neo-Freudians' views of order leads to the following conclusions: (1) order must be seen as part of the cultural context; (2) order involves a progression toward fulfilling goals and actualizing one's potentials; and (3) order derives from individual choices and directions. This view of order is one which focuses on a high level of wellness; it goes beyond an ability to meet the basic requirements of life.

VIEW OF DISORDER

The view of disorder that is described by the neo-Freudians is dominated by a focus on neurotic behavior. Neuroses, in general, are seen as resulting from a constricting or rigid approach to life in which the individual inflexibly approaches new situations with old behavioral and cognitive patterns. Further, disordered behavior is seen to differ from order more in degree than in kind. These neo-Freudians place varying amounts of emphasis on the role of interpersonal conflict, or anxiety, in precipitating neurotic behavior, but they agree that the primary manifestation of neurotic behavior is difficulty in interpersonal relationships.

In Adler's conceptualization, disorder arises from a faulty or constricting life-style (i.e., the individual's cognitive plan for coping with life) or from the choices for action made within the context of the life-style. The same life-style can lead to useful or useless behavior; however, disorder occurs when the individual makes poor behavioral choices within the frame of the life-style. On the other hand, the life-style itself may be the source of disorder.[5] A constricting life-style is one which is rigid and limiting in terms of the individual's goals and behavioral repertoire. However, even a constricting life-style (for example, one in which the individual refuses to take risks or experiment with new ways of behaving) will not necessarily cause problems of living, unless it is challenged by reality.[5]

A faulty life-style is organized around certain distorted perceptions. There are six categories of distortions, or "basic mistakes," that people may hold: distorted attitudes about one's self and capabilities; distorted attitudes about the world and people; distorted goals, such as "I must be perfect"; distorted methods of achieving goals; distorted ideas about life; and distorted conclusions about other people or about what will happen in particular situations.[1] These distorted beliefs reflect faulty learning or the avoidance of common sense.

Adler introduced the notion of an inferiority complex. When individuals feel inferior—socially or biologically—they subsequently compensate by over-emphasizing some other trait or tendency. Adler was less concerned with the role of anxiety than other neo-Freudians. He acknowledged that anxiety would contribute to the development of neurotic behavior, primarily through the possibility of leading to the overemphasis of certain behavioral responses (those which were not anxiety-provoking to the individual) at the expense of others.

One of Horney's major contributions to understanding disorder was to locate neurotic behavior within a cultural context. She asserted that neurotic behavior was culturally relevant, and that what might be considered neurotic in one society would not necessarily be so in another. For her, neurotic disorders were characterized by rigidity and compulsiveness, that is, the indiscriminate application of one response to many events. The inflexibility of these responses prevents realization of the person's potential.

Horney placed the development of disorder in infancy, with the experience of basic anxiety. The need to overcome this anxiety leads to three categories of interpersonal responses: moving toward people or seeking safety in relationships; moving away from people—becoming self-reliant; and moving against people—rejecting the advances or advice of others.[6] Whereas the normal person achieves a balance among these responses, the neurotic prefers and

41

uses one pattern exclusively. Succeeding in the use of one pattern, however, means repressing the needs that relate to the unchosen patterns while idealizing the needs of the predominating pattern. For instance, the person who always moves toward people might believe that there is virtue in passively acquiescing to others' wishes and not making waves. This imbalance of interpersonal responses inevitably leads to conflict between the person's idealized self and "actual" self. This conflict cannot be resolved until the person recognizes the *ideal* self as neurotic.

Thus, Horney's view of disorder involves an overly rigid set of behavioral responses that concentrate on one mode of interpersonal relationships to the exclusion of others. This condition, precipitated by childhood anxiety, prevents development of potential in adult life and eventually leads to conflict within the person.

Sullivan also believed that disorder represented attempts to overcome or dispel anxiety.[2] This anxiety might be elicited by proximity to anxious or malevolent persons, rejection, ridicule, punishment in a malevolent context, and inconsistencies of significant adults. In these situations, the child first responds with avoidance and later ceases to use behaviors relevant to such situations. For instance, a child who is ridiculed for something said in school may eventually stop speaking up in class. When the child cannot avoid these settings, or needs to use behaviors that are associated with settings in order to reduce need tensions, conflict develops. The conflict may be handled by substituting ineffective behaviors, by selective inattention to situations that cannot be physically ignored, or by mental preoccupations that preclude the possibility of making the distressing responses. The child ridiculed in school might thus begin to act the role of clown, not pay attention to the teacher, or daydream during class. The consequences of these attempts at conflict resolution are a constricted life-style, interference with interpersonal relationships that are necessary to satisfying needs, ineffectiveness in interpersonal relationships, and dissociation or deletion of certain responses from one's behavioral repertoire.

Sullivan, along with Adler and Horney, therefore traced disorder to a life-style dominated by one set of behavioral responses at the expense of others. Sullivan considered that the anxiety that resulted from inconsistencies or rejection in interpersonal situations was a crucial factor in leading to a rigid life-style and future inability to satisfy interpersonal needs.

Fromm considered neurosis to be more a philosophical than a clinical dilemma, although he did delineate various neurotic character types. He viewed neurosis as the outcome of the individual's fear of freedom and corresponding choice of a nonproductive orientation to life. An example of a nonproductive orientation is the "receptive" orientation, dominated by the need to conform and the belief that experts exist to tell one how to do things. Fromm believed that certain character orientations were more likely to be found in particular societies and at particular times than others. For instance, the receptive orientation is more often found in societies with social inequities, where one group or class habitually exploits the rights of another.[3] The marketing orientation, in which the person experiences and evaluates himself and others as a salable commodity, is a product of modern times. Thus, in his view, disorder is closely tied to the meanings available in a given culture. Society provides both the conflict and the modes for its expression in the neurotic personality.

In their views of disorder, the neo-Freudians, with the exception of Adler, did not wholly reject the notion of biological drives and tension reduction as motivating behavior. However, they sought new ways to encapsulate this concept—for instance, as a need for safety or a need for security and well-being. In addition, they included with this need an inherent urge toward actualization of one's potentials or inner self. Disorder was then seen as impinging upon this actualization and creating conflict between the realities and possibilities of one's life. The neo-Freudians considered social and environmental circumstances to be crucial factors in determining whether or not a constricting or actualizing life-style would develop. Finally, the concept of conflict, a classical Freudian concept, continues to dominate this view of disorder. The neo-Freudians ultimately remain true to their heritage by linking their conception of disorder to thwarted drives, distorted response patterns, and intrapersonal conflict.

ACTION IMPLICATIONS

The neo-Freudians as a whole realized that classical psychoanalytic treatment was too inflexible to be used for all patients. In particular, they objected to emphasis on daily or almost daily treatment, the establishment of a transference neurosis as a vital part of treatment, and the operating criterion of free association.[7] Because of their common belief that behavior was learned in interpersonal relationships, they saw the therapeutic setting as a special class of interpersonal relationships in which the therapist's behavior contributed actively to the patient's learning.

Adler conceptualized the therapeutic process as an educational experience potentially involving more than one therapist and more than one patient. The goal of this cooperative process was to develop the patient's interest and investment in social relationships.[5]

He delineated four aims of therapy that have since been expanded upon by his followers. The first aim of therapy was to strive for a friendly relationship between equals. To achieve this, it was necessary for the therapist and patient to align their goals. This meant that the therapist could not arbitrarily determine treatment goals for the patient and that the patient might have to modify or clarify his or her own initial plans for therapy. Therefore, the model for the therapeutic relationship could not be based on the medical model (see Chapter 1), which posited a relationship in which the therapist directed the course of treatment because of his or her superior knowledge and understanding of pathology while the patient willingly complied with the suggested treatment.

Second, since the ultimate goal of therapy concerned the development of social interest, therapy investigated the patient's life-style and how it affected current functioning. Because the life-style is dynamic, the client's current behavior in the context of the therapeutic setting was as relevant as his or her history. In fact, the importance of childhood recollections lay in their ability to enhance understanding of the life-style. Because people tend to sift through their past, selectively remembering only those incidents that are consistent with their present life-style, memories served as clues to understanding the life-style of the patient.[5] Free association was discouraged by Adler, but he believed that dreams offered relevant material. However, unlike Freud's notion of dreams as replays of old problems, in Adlerian therapy dreams are viewed as problem solving or rehearsing for the future.[5]

The third aim of Adlerian therapy was to achieve insight, or "understanding translated into constructive action" (p. 70).[5] The therapist might use interpretation or explanation of the patient's behavior, humor, parables, and paradox to facilitate insight. Paradox, also used by communication/interaction theorists and logotherapists (see Chapters 4 and 8), involves a seemingly contradictory statement or situation, which, through its inherent contradictions, leads to understanding or to the desired behavior. Telling someone afraid of fainting in public places to deliberately faint the next time he or she enters a store is an example of paradoxical treatment.

The last step in Adlerian therapy was reorientation, or taking the risk to change. Reorientation involves "motivation-modification" (p. 100),[2] that is, establishing new or more realistic goals for behavior and identifying new or more functional alternatives to one's present actions.

Contemporary Adlerians use a variety of techniques, including role playing, role modeling by the therapist, setting either achievable or paradoxical tasks for the client, group therapy, therapeutic social clubs, and marriage and family counseling.[1,5]

Horney's descriptions of the therapeutic process seem quite conservative and not substantially different from classical analysis. She emphasized the development of insight and understanding by clients in recognizing their response patterns, their ineffectiveness, and their relationship to symptoms.

Free association was an important part of the patient's role, and "observation, understanding, interpretation, help in resistance, and general human help" were the mainstay of the therapist's role (p. 511).[2]

In her later writings, Horney specified a set of four therapeutic goals: (1) assumption of responsibility for one's actions and decisions; (2) inner dependence, or recognition of and belief in one's own hierarchy of values; (3) spontaneity of feeling; and (4) wholeheartedness, or a total commitment to one's feelings, work, and beliefs.[2]

Sullivan, along with Adler and Horney, believed that although childhood socialization needed to be examined to discern the roots of anxiety, subsequent maladaptive thinking and behavior patterns needed to be directly attacked in therapy. In particular, Sullivan considered the "psychiatric interview," or treatment session, to represent an interpersonal relationship between the client and therapist. As a member of this relationship, the therapist both contributed to and responded to the client's behaviors. Sullivan called the therapist a "participant-observer" to denote this role as a cause of, respondent to, and observer of the client's behavior.[2]

Sullivan conceptualized the psychiatric interview as a single session or a series of sessions, consisting of four stages. In the first stage, or inception, observation was the primary function of the therapist. Even at this early point, however, Sullivan thought that clients should feel they are learning something. The second stage, or reconnaissance, referred to the gathering of extensive and intensive biographical material. Following the reconnaissance, the therapist would proceed with detailed inquiry, or the testing of hypotheses about how the person might think, act, or feel in various situations. Finally, the interview should be terminated with suggestions for future problem solving on the client's part.[4]

Fromm's picture of therapy was, in a sense, that of a religion, with its ultimate goal being to remove the individual's "blocks to loving and being loved" and to resolve his or her "strictures on productivity and creativity" (p. 211).[7] To this end, the therapist's role was to help the client understand irrational needs for authority by examining the relationship with the therapist. In this process, the client would discover healthy parts of the self that had been condemned or ignored by the patient.[7]

Again, we see that the neo-Freudians both diverged from and converged with classical psychoanalysis. Therapy, for the most part, involves a verbal session in which the client presents information about the present and past and the therapist interprets this information in order to help the client develop new ways of satisfying interpersonal needs. Unlike classical psychoanalysts, the neo-Freudians believed that the client's current functioning within the context of the treatment session was as important a source of material as past history for analysis. Neo-Freudians were both directive in their approach—by their willingness to give suggestions, to guide the course of the session, and to acknowledge their impact on the client's behavior—and cooperative, in their emphasis on sharing responsibility for setting goals.

CRITICISMS AND LIMITATIONS

Neo-Freudians have been subject to criticisms from both classical psychoanalysts and writers outside the psychoanalytic tradition. Orthodox analysts criticize the neo-Freudians for substituting Freud's libido theory with equally ambiguous concepts, such as Horney's "real," "ideal," and "actual" selves. According to one writer, "there is a tendency to recast Freudian formulations in novel, excruciatingly complicated neologisms; to concentrate on nuances, torturing these into broad theorems" (p. 220).[7] The neo-Freudians have been further criticized for tendencies to overgeneralize.[2] Adler, for instance, attributes all behavior to one ultimate fictional goal, while Horney regards large organizational sets of behavior responses as obvious and clearly cohesive response patterns.[2]

The neo-Freudians are ambivalent about the role of biological drives, and while they postulate a motive or force toward self-actualization, their treatment of it as an unconscious drive seems more similar to libido theory than to concepts of effectance motivation or intrinsic motivation. The latter concepts propose that the individual engages in activity in order to feel effective and competent in his or her environment. In this sense, although an innate drive, effectance motivation involves conscious decisions on the individual's part. The neo-Freudians' drive toward self-actualization seems closer in spirit to an unconscious force that determines behavior by virtue of its being unimpeded by external events.

Although refusing to attribute behavior to either solely intrinsic or solely extrinsic determinants, the neo-Freudians nevertheless remain elusive about the ways in which a person might respond to or act on the environment. This major limitation seems to come from their position as a bridge between orthodox Freudian theory and environmental/sociological perspectives on behavior. Not willing to totally give up the constructs of psychoanalysis, they were unable to resolve some of the paradoxes that Freudian theory had raised for them. Thus, although they rejected the mechanistic view of the mind proposed by Freud, they did not reject the most fundamental mechanistic ideas underlying Freudian thought. Retaining the notion of an unconscious force that drives persons to act perpetuated the view of persons as tension-releasing organisms. In some ways their work resembles a situation in which theorists attempt to resolve problems within a dominant paradigm of theory by revision of that theory, when what is really required is a major reorientation

46

and shift in fundamental views and precepts. The work of the neo-Freudians is therefore more like surface or cosmetic repair than reconstruction and reconceptualization.

COMMENTARY

The impact of neo-Freudian thinking on occupational therapy has been more subtle than that of classical psychoanalytic thinking. Because psychiatrists have continued to dominate mental health settings, as they have incorporated the ideas of the neo-Freudians, other mental health workers have been under pressure to do so as well. To the extent that this has meant an increasing awareness of sociocultural influences on psychosocial order and disorder, this has been beneficial to occupational therapy.

Likewise, the contributions of neo-Freudians to understanding the goal-oriented nature of the person and the importance of work in giving meaning to life supports the concept that the purpose of occupational therapy is broader than activity prescribed for symptom relief (i.e., reduction of anxiety). That is, they pave the way for asserting that occupations can be used to reach goals, generate meaning, and so on. Interestingly, the development of these kinds of themes in occupational therapy have not relied on neo-Freudian thought, but rather on the work of humanistic/existential writers and ego psychologists. This may be because the most fundamental Freudian tenets remain intact in neo-Freudian thought, producing a deep incompatibility with occupational therapy. Thus, if one does not closely examine the bases of these theories, they may appear more overtly similar to current occupational therapy than they really are. It should be noted, for example, that the occupational therapy view of order and disorder that we describe in this text is substantially different from that of the neo-Freudians. Issues that form the crux of occupational therapy thinking, such as locus of control, effectance motivation, and maintenance of habits of work, leisure, and self-care in everyday life, are virtually ignored by the neo-Freudians. Similarly, the techniques used by neo-Freudians have mostly continued in the mainstream of other psychoanalytic techniques. Verbal, insight-oriented therapy is radically different from the action-oriented techniques used by occupational therapists.

SUMMARY

History and Purpose	Adler broke with Freud to found a school of Interpersonal Psychology, setting the stage for dissension by other pscyhoanalysts.
	Horney and Sullivan each developed theoretical systems emphasizing cultural and interpersonal determinants of mental health.
	Fromm incorporated existential, sociological, and psychoanalytic ideas into a perspective on psychosocial order.
	Neo-Freudians as a whole protested Freudian drive theory and its mechanistic view of personality.
View of Order	Human behavior is culturally embedded and environmentally nurtured. Behavior is unified and integrated.
	Adler's view of order stresses an altruistic and goal-oriented life-style.
	Horney stresses the ability to reconcile one's ideal and actual selves in order to allow "real" self to become actualized.
	Sullivan emphasizes the role of interpersonal relationships in letting the child (or adult) develop psychological order.
	Fromm emphasizes coming to terms with historical and existential crises in order to live productively.
Disorder	Generally, neo-Freudians believe that disorder is precipitated by childhood anxiety; their focus is on neurotic behavior.
	Social and cultural conditions contribute to the development of neurotic behavior.
	Neuroses are manifested in poor interpersonal relationships, the use of one pattern or mode of behavior responses for all experiences, and the inability to satisfy personal needs.

Action Implications	Behavior is learned in the context of interpersonal relationships; the therapeutic setting is a type of interpersonal relationship.
	The therapist responds to, causes, and observes the client's behavior; the relationship between client and therapist is as important a source of information as is past history.
	The therapeutic process is an educational experience with the goals of understanding and changing one's life-style, setting more realistic goals for action, and becoming committed to one's feelings, work, and to other people.
Criticisms and Limitations	Neo-Freudians introduced complicated new terminology whose meanings may not differ very much from Freudian concepts.
	The neo-Freudians postulate a force toward self-actualization, but they treat it as an unconscious drive similar to Freud's concept of libidinal drive.
	Their contributions tend to be surface or cosmetic repair to Freudian ideas.
Commentary	Emphasis on goal-oriented nature of persons and importance of work in giving meaning to life is compatible with a view of occupational therapy as being more than tension reduction.
	Neo-Freudian theories for the most part ignore themes that are crucial to occupational therapy theory.
	Fundamental Freudian tenets, left intact in neo-Freudian thinking, are incompatible with occupational therapy.

TERMS AND CONCEPTS

actual self   the way in which a person is experienced and perceived by others.

bad me   behaviors or experiences that the child associates with anxiety.

faulty life-style	one in which the individual's choices for action are limited, due to distorted perceptions or beliefs about oneself, other people, and life.
free association	the process of making the unconscious conscious by having the person report all thoughts, uncensored and regardless of their seeming insignificance.
good me	behaviors or experiences that the child associates with feelings of security.
ideal self	the way a person thinks he or she should "ideally" be.
life-style	a primarily nonconscious plan for coping with life events that includes an ideal image of oneself, and a hierarchy of goals or priorities for action.
parataxic mode	pattern of thinking in which cause and effect of events is based solely on their sequential occurrence.
phenomenological psychology	the study of behavior from the perspective of the individual's experience; a person's behaviors cannot be understood without understanding this person's interpretations and personal framework for these behaviors.
private logic	a complex of personally held beliefs that direct an individual's life goals.
prototaxic mode	pattern of thought in which the child (individual) does not perceive self as separate from the environment.
psychiatric interview	Sullivan's conceptualization of the treatment session, as well as a series of sessions. In both cases, the psychiatric interview moves through four stages, from observation to data gathering, to detailed inquiry, to suggestions for future problem solving.
real self	one's central being, which, given appropriate conditions, becomes actualized by the individual.
social interest	a desire and tendency to cooperate with other people for the good of society.

syntaxic mode	pattern of thought characterized by logic, reasoning, and the use of publicly accepted symbols.
transference	the emotional bond that forms between the therapist and client; the client begins to relate to the therapist as though the therapist were another significant person in the client's life.

REFERENCES

1. Dinkmeyer, D. C., Pew, W. L., & Dinkmeyer, D. C., Jr. *Adlerian counseling and psychotherapy*. Monterey, Calif.: Brooks/Cole, 1979.
2. Ford, D. H., & Urban, H. B. *Systems of psychotherapy: A comparative study*. New York: Wiley, 1963.
3. Fromm, E. *Man for himself*. New York: Holt, Rinehart & Winston, 1947.
4. Harper, R. A. *Psychoanalysis and psychotherapy: 36 systems*. New York: Jason Aaronson, 1974.
5. Mosak, H. H. Adlerian psychotherapy. In R. J. Corsini (Ed.), *Current psychotherapies* (2nd ed.). Itasca, Ill.: Peacock, 1979.
6. Munroe, R. A. *Schools of psychoanalytic thought*. New York: Holt, Rinehart & Winston, 1955.
7. Wolberg, L. R. *The technique of psychotherapy. Part one* (3rd ed.). New York: Grune & Stratton, 1977.
8. Wyss, D. *Psychoanalytic schools from the beginning to the present*. New York: Jason Aaronson, 1973.

ADDITIONAL READINGS

Adler, A. *The practice and theory of individual psychology*. New York: Harcourt, Brace, 1924.

Adler, A. *Social interest*. New York: Putnam, 1939.

Clinebell, H. *Contemporary growth therapies*. Nashville: Abingdon, 1981.

Fromm, E. *The sane society*. New York: Rinehart, 1955.

Horney, K. *Neurosis and human growth*. New York: Norton, 1950.

Progoff, I. *The death and rebirth of psychology*. New York: Julian Press, 1956.

Sullivan, H. S. *The interpersonal theory of psychiatry*. New York: Norton, 1953.

Sullivan, H. S. *The psychiatric interview*. New York: Norton, 1954.

4

Existential-Humanist Bodies of Thought

The existential-humanist tradition is united by a fundamental vision of the nature of human existence. Logotherapy, client-centered therapy, humanistic and existential psychotherapy, gestalt therapy, and the human potential movement all have been influenced by existential and phenomenological philosophy, and all share a concern for helping the individual to find meaning in life. The differences among these approaches result primarily from the emphases of the key individual associated with each body of knowledge: Carl Rogers with client-centered therapy, Victor Frankl with logotherapy, Abraham Maslow with humanistic psychology. Inevitably, these pairings have led to the association of special techniques with particular streams of thought. Therefore, while the overall goals for each of these psychosocial therapies may be similar, their action implications often differ.

Because of the concern for helping the individual to transcend the "givens" of life,[2] the target of these therapies is rarely the psychotic patient, the chronically mentally ill, or the deinstitutionalized schizophrenic. These therapies do not focus on symptom relief, nor are they concerned with the development of adaptive daily living skills per se. Instead, they attempt to fill a spiritual gap believed to be ignored by psychotherapy. What Frankl says of logotherapy is essentially true for all the existential-humanistic approaches:

> Logotherapy must *supplement* psychotherapy. . . . By the use of logotherapy we are equipped to deal with philosophical questions within their own frame of reference, and can embark on objective discussion of the spiritual distress of human beings suffering from psychic disturbances. (p. 17)[6]

Because its target is the spiritual or existential dissatisfaction and alienation of individuals in modern society, existential-humanistic psychology has been applied to the parts of society that may contribute to or potentially alleviate this distress—industry and education—as well as to psychotherapy.[10]

This chapter covers the general themes of the existential-humanist tradition and highlights Frankl's logotherapy and Rogers' client-centered therapy. These two therapies are emphasized because of the unique action implications of logotherapy and the particular relevance of Frankl's discussion of meaning to occupational therapy, and because of Rogers' pervasive influence on helping professionals' relationship and interviewing techniques.

A semantic problem arises in this chapter in that the terms *existential* and *humanistic* have been used by different writers to refer to both disparate bodies of knowledge and to one tradition. This chapter, when referring to general themes, will use both terms in a hyphenated form; when referring to specific contributions from either school of thought the appropriate term will be used alone.

HISTORY AND PURPOSE

Drawing on phenomenology, existential philosophy, and humanistic themes in philosophy, literature, and religion, existential-humanistic psychology arose in response to mechanistic and reductionist currents in twentieth century psychology. These trends ignored the inner experience of humans and sought generalizations about human behavior from the study of rats and pigeons.[10,14] Existential-humanistic psychology attempted to counterbalance these trends by stressing the importance of understanding human experience from each individual's perspective, that is, by understanding the personal meaning that an individual attaches to behavior.

William James and G. Stanley Hall, two nineteenth century American psychologists, are usually identified as early humanists because of their belief that psychology should stress the wholeness, unique passions, and individuality of persons.[14] This orientation was later reiterated in the 1930s by Goldstein, Allport, and Maslow. Significantly, the period prior and subsequent to World War II was a time when many European scholars emigrated to the United States. These scholars brought with them a school of thought—phenomenology—that stressed the importance of subjectivity and intuition as the keys to understanding a person's experience and knowledge of the world.[10] In other words, knowledge, according to phenomenologists, not only differs for each person, but is also continually shaped by each individual's experiences and subsequent interpretations of these experiences. The influence of this philosophy was felt in terms of the methods used to study behavior—phenomenology emphasized the unbiased recording of human experience from the subject's perspective, rather than the objective description of external, observable behavior.

During this period, existentialism was also attracting many adherents. Resting on a phenomenological foundation, existentialism focused on the individual's subjective awareness of existence and the way in which one came to terms with the knowledge of one's inevitable nonexistence (death).[10] In Europe, Binswanger was one of the first psychoanalysts to examine patients' experiences in terms of existential issues. He did not, however, develop a comprehensive system of therapy, so although he may be considered a "founder" of existential analysis, his influence is less directly felt today.[11]

Frankl, another European therapist, is associated with a specific form of existential therapy—logotherapy. Logotherapy clearly reflects Frankl's personal history. Before World War II, Frankl was the medical director of a large mental hospital. During the war, imprisoned in a Nazi concentration camp, he struggled to find meaning in suffering and to retain the freedom to choose his attitude toward his fate. The idea that freedom remains in the most dire of circumstances was to become a central concept of logotherapy.

In the 1950s, several Americans were responsible for the systematic application of existential principles to psychology. Rollo May, James Bugental, and Carl Rogers particularly helped to consolidate the existential-humanistic movement. Rogers was profoundly influenced by Otto Rank's conceptualization of the treatment process. For Rank, the therapist's qualities as a human being and the relationship with the patient far outweighed the therapist's technical skills in guiding the patient toward health.[9] Building on this, Rogers proposed a nondirective, person-centered form of therapy, which for many individuals came to epitomize existential-humanist psychology.

In the 1950s and 1960s certain sociocultural trends further contributed to the emergence of the existential-humanist movement as a viable school of psychology.[14] The increasing alienation of people from their feelings and from their communities, the loss of tradition and continuity in modern life, and the compartmentalization of life, fostered by the domination of technology all fueled both the 1960s counterculture movement and existential-humanist psychology. Both groups espoused many of the same values—freedom, authenticity, and openness to experience and to others. Existential-humanist psychology perceived itself as offering individuals a chance to reconnect with themselves and with each other. To this end, sensitivity groups and encounter groups, which brought people together to examine their interpersonal behavior in intensive group experiences, became the cultural panacea of the 1960s.[14]

Many of the more unorthodox forms of therapy such as the marathon encounter groups which proliferated in the 1960s under the auspices of humanism and the human potential movement are no longer in vogue. Existential-humanist psychology, nevertheless, continues to be a strong force today.

VIEW OF ORDER

Three themes are central to the view of order in the existential-humanist body of knowledge: the urge toward wholeness, intentionality, and authenticity in one's relationships. The urge toward wholeness describes the belief that behavior is motivated by something more than unconscious drives or needs. Although not denying the presence of these needs, this body of knowledge sees the ultimate motivation as being an urge for unity and wholeness, manifested in the individual's search for self-actualization.[14]

The phenomenological focus of this tradition and its emphasis on an innate drive toward self-actualization converge in the concept of "intentionality." Intentionality refers to the idea that our experiences, and our perceptions of these experiences, derive from our goals or intentions.[14] In other words, not only do we have our own private interpretations of our experiences, but our personal intentions or goals lead us to choose these experiences in the first place.

Authenticity in one's relationship comes from the willingness to remain open to experience and to others and to not see oneself or others as fixed, immutable entities.[11,14] This authenticity is difficult to achieve, however, because of our awareness of conditions of "nonbeing." Conditions of nonbeing that fill us with existential anxiety are death, the realization that ultimately we are all alone, and a sense of meaninglessness in what we do. Existential anxiety is common to everyone; what determines order (or disorder) is the individual's response to it. The "ordered" individual is one who, despite this existential anxiety, persists in the active pursuit of goals that will lead to self-actualization. In this way, the individual achieves authenticity as well.[11,14]

Logotherapy and client-centered therapy incorporate and extend these central tenets, each in its own way. Although logotherapy draws on fundamental existential concepts, Frankl stated that it goes further because it is concerned not just with *being*, but also with *meaning*. For logotherapy, the person's life is dominated by the goal of finding meaning.[4]

Logotherapy bases its philosophy on three assumptions: freedom of will, an innate will to meaning, and the phenomenological meaning of life.[7,16] The first, freedom of will, is a freedom within the constraints or conditions of one's existence. People can assert themselves and take responsibility for their actions, or if they cannot choose their actions, then they can take responsibility for their attitudes. This freedom implies a moral responsibility of the individual, either to society, to religious beliefs, or to one's own conscience.[7]

The "will to meaning" is not a drive or need, but an innate search that shapes one's life. Meaning is found through the discovery of values that are relevant to one's life and through the commitment to a cause of greater significance than one's immediate, daily, and personal concerns.[7] Frankl's attitude toward self-actualization differs from other existential-humanists in that he does not consider it to be a motivating force, but an effect: Self-actualization and pleasure may result from the search for meaning, but they cannot be obtained as long as they are directly pursued as ends in and of themselves. According to Frankl, then, psychosocial order does not come from the pursuit of self-actualization but from the attainment of meaning.

The third assumption of logotherapy is that meaning is experienced subjectively and, therefore, differently for each person. There are three ways in which life may become meaningful for the individual:

> First, through *what we give* to life (in terms of our creative works); second, by *what we take* from the world (in terms of our experiencing values); and third, through the *stand we take* toward a fate we no longer can change (an incurable disease, an inoperable cancer, or the like). (p. 15)[7]

For Frankl, existential anxiety comes from the doubt that life has meaning and the tension that is created by the gap between existence and the *essence* or meaning of one's existence. This tension is a vital part of being human and is resolved by directing one's life toward a commitment or significant goal.[7]

Client-centered therapy is essentially a theory describing the optimal conditions for growth in human development and in the therapeutic relationship. Rogers' view of human order shares with Frankl's an emphasis on values and the individual's subjective experiences, but it has little to say about meaning or existential anxiety. Rogers' first interest was in the creation of an empathetic, therapeutic environment, and his theory of personality, derived from his observations of the therapeutic relationship, reflects the same emphasis.[12,14]

Maslow's hierarchy of needs is central to Rogers' view of development.[9] Maslow postulated the existence of five levels of needs. The first three levels comprise "deficiency" needs, needs that are essential for immediate maintenance of the organism. These include physiological and safety needs, and the need to belong to a social group and to be loved. The higher two levels, termed "metaneeds," are long-term and forever active. These are the needs for esteem and for self-actualization. The salience and potency of each level changes with the person's time of life, environmental circumstances, and so on, but generally, the individual will not concentrate on higher level needs until lower levels are met. Rogers believed, as did Maslow, that psychosocial order represented the realization of these higher level needs.

According to Rogers, the organism has a basic, innate goal to grow and enhance and actualize its capacities. Through this process, the individual develops an increasingly differentiated self-concept. As the individual interacts with the environment and with other people, new experiences are either perceived and organized in some relationship to oneself, or ignored and distorted. Rejection or distortion of these perceptions occurs because they are inconsistent with the view of self that one has begun to hold, whereas the acceptance of perceptions occurs when these are consistent with one's self-image. For instance, an adolescent girl who thinks of herself as unattractive may ignore feedback from family or friends that contradicts her self-image. On the other hand, if she sees herself as possibly being in an awkward stage, yet going through a process of growth and change, then she may be able to accept feedback from others on both her strengths and weaknesses. Consequently, for psychosocial order to exist, the person must have a flexible and realistic self-image that allows for the assimilation of new experiences. For the child, this will occur naturally when the parent's love has been unconditional, or not selectively given and withdrawn according to what behaviors the child exhibits.[12]

In Rogers' view of human order, individuals will naturally value such ideas as freedom, communality, and respect for others, unless they are contaminated by the false values of other people. Well-adjusted persons, however, being open to new experiences and constantly reexamining their perceptions of these experiences, will not hold fixed, rigid values, but will realize that valuing is an ongoing process.

The overall view of order in the existential-humanist tradition is one in which the individual makes responsible choices for action in the face of a universal sense of aloneness and meaninglessness in life. These decisions to act reflect an innate motivation for self-actualization and the individual's subjective interpretation of experience. Finally, self-actualization and meaning in life come from and imply a willingness to remain flexible and open in one's attitudes toward and perceptions of others, experiences, and oneself.

Rogers and Frankl are both clearly in the existential-humanist tradition; yet their theories diverge from one another in significant ways. The most important difference between the two theories is the emphasis Frankl gives to meaning. Rogers' belief in the self-actualizing tendency of the person fits more closely with the tradition as a whole. For Frankl, the need for self-actualization is not enough to shape one's life; it is the will to meaning that makes life more than just mere existence.

VIEW OF DISORDER

Existential anxiety is an inevitable component of life; the way one faces this anxiety, however, can create psychopathology. Lying, or not admitting to oneself that death and finitude are ultimately part of life, results in neurotic as opposed to existential anxiety. Existential anxiety is an inescapable response to our awareness of death; neurotic anxiety, however, is an unrealistic response that arises from an attempt to deny our eventual aloneness and the certainty of death.[11] Herein lies a paradox, however, because to some extent, denial of the conditions of nonbeing is precisely what enables people to live a "normal" life:

> The individual has to protect himself against the world, and he can do this only as any other animal would: by narrowing down the world, shutting off experience, developing an obliviousness both to the terrors of the world and to his own anxieties. . . . We can say that the essence of normality is the *refusal of reality*. (p. 178)[1]

Persons who are called neurotic, though, have carried this denial too far: they have chosen a life-style that has so many restrictions and limitations that they can no longer make active choices or grow in their understanding of themselves and their lives.[1]

In Frankl's perspective, disorder comes from the loss of meaning in life.[6] As with existential anxiety, the loss of meaning is precipitated both by our awareness of the conditions of nonbeing and our unwillingness to accept responsibility for the way in which we respond to these conditions. Frankl hypothesizes that this loss of meaning, or the existential vacuum, is a con- comitant of industrialization, which contributes to the meaninglessness of work[6] and to unemployment. He notes: "Having no work, [a person] thinks life has no meaning. . . . Unemployment becomes a culture medium for the proliferation of neuroses" (p. 121).[6]

Despite this abstract view of disorder, Frankl describes two very concrete forms of neurotic behavior: anticipatory anxiety and excessive self-observa- tion, or excessive intention. When someone fears that he or she will stammer or sweat during a speech, the anticipation of this is enough to bring about precisely what the person has dreaded will happen; this is anticipatory anxiety.[7] Excessive self-observation or excessive intention have the opposite effect— the more one wants to achieve a certain state, the more it eludes the person. (It is for this reason that Frankl states that one cannot pursue pleasure or self-actualization as ends in themselves.)

Rogers' discussion of disorder is quite discrepant from the existentialists' and does not relate pathology to a conscious decision to lie to oneself about life experiences or to a loss of meaning. Instead, he attributes it to a tragic development in infancy.[11] When the parent's love is conditionally given for certain behaviors and attitudes, the child soon becomes estranged from the characteristics or behaviors that are not rewarded by the parents. These behaviors are pushed out of the self-concept or the child's idealized self- image, because to admit them would mean admitting that certain parts of the child were not valued or loved by the parents. Further, the child develops certain defensive reactions or mechanisms that make it possible to ignore experiences that are incongruent with this self-image. As long as people are able to ignore incongruous information, they will not feel internal conflict or seek therapy. Once someone begins to admit that there is substantial contradictory evidence to the self-image, internal tension will begin to grow.[12]

Rogers is more concerned with *why* someone will feel discomfort than with what the manifestations of this discomfort may be. Similarly, the connections between neurotic anxiety, the existential vacuum, and the development of specific pathological behavior are somewhat unclear. While the concepts of existential and neurotic anxiety are intuitively meaningful, why they should result in particular symptoms is less so. In both cases, the avoidance of a clear-cut discussion of pathology no doubt reflects the focus of this body of knowledge on the phenomenological meaning of existence. In addition, the strong philosophical background of the existential-humanist tradition is probably responsible for the rather nonclinical approach it presents to disorder.

ACTION IMPLICATIONS

Existential-humanist therapy is characterized by four distinguishing features. These are:

1. a concern for the autonomous, "being" aspects of the client;
2. emphasis on the here-and-now experiences of both the client and the therapist;
3. the belief that the existential quest (whether for self-actualization or finding meaning in life) is as important as any instinctual needs or drives; and
4. a focus on the "real" aspects of the therapeutic relationship, not just its transference aspects.[14]

Taken together, these features imply the overall goal of helping the client to achieve an authentic existence, one in which the individual can dynamically and openly "be" in the physical and social worlds and in his or her own personal world.

Traditionally, specific techniques have been deemphasized by the existential-humanists. They believe that to do otherwise leads to treating the client as an object in a treatment category, with the therapist deciding on the best means for changing the client.[11] In actuality, many existentialists draw on psychoanalytic techniques, but they differ from classical analysis primarily in their belief that the client has the right to freely choose to be influenced by or to resist the therapist. In addition, the therapist and client recognize that meaning is not absolute and that it may differ for each of them.[14]

Although Rogers' client-centered therapy embodies these beliefs, he strongly felt that components of the ideal therapeutic relationship could and should be identified and that the model for this relationship was not classical analysis. Rogers' dominant interest has been in the creation of an environment in which the client would feel safe to explore unwanted perceptions and to reorganize his or her life structure in a less defensive fashion. To this end, client-centered therapy involves a process in which the client, unsettled by the contradictions between his or her experiences and self-concept, finds that both the certain and uncertain parts of self are accepted by the therapist. This acceptance offers clients the freedom to reexamine self-perceptions and shape a new self-concept.[12] Clients change because within the context of a genuine, empathic relationship with the therapist, they are able to achieve a new self-awareness and see that both their right and wrong decisions, their certainties and uncertainties, can be accepted by another person.

Positive regard, one of the key elements in this relationship, is a form of liking and respect for another person that acknowledges one's individuality and does not trivialize a person's feelings. Another important aspect of the relationship is the feedback provided by the therapist. Although Rogers initially conceptualized the therapist's role as being nondirective, more recently he has come to believe that the therapist's feedback is useful in helping the client process information or attend to things that might otherwise have been screened out.[11] Congruence, another key therapeutic element, refers to the therapist's attempts to share subjective reactions to the client with the client. In other words, the therapist does not maintain a facade, but allows his or her true responses to be perceived by the client. Only in this way can the therapist and client relate to one another as unique individuals, rather than as objects. Finally, the therapist also helps the client begin to process his or her experiences in a more vital, evocative, and potent language. As the client's mode of expression becomes more enhancing and actualizing, experiences become so as well.[11]

Logotherapy means "therapy through meaning" (p. 11).[4] In some respects, logotherapy is more unusual than other existential therapies. First, Frankl is careful to note that logotherapy is not intended for all problems and that it can be a supplement to other types of treatment. Second, logotherapy is girded by the belief that engaging in meaningful activity may be the most effective form of therapy for people confronting an existential vacuum.[13] Third, it has developed two unique tools that stand somewhat apart from the rest of the existential tradition. *Paradoxical intention** and *dereflection*, specifically applied

---

*The use of paradox in therapy is not unique to logotherapy; this technique is also discussed in Chapters 3 and 8.

to the problems of anticipatory anxiety and excessive intention, are considered to be effective treatment tools because of people's ability to step back and be detached from their behaviors. Through the use of paradoxical intention, the person is able "to develop a sense of detachment toward his neurosis by laughing at it" (p. 147).[6] Paradoxical intention encourages the client to do precisely what is feared, while dereflection encourages the person to be less self-observant and to ignore the trouble. Instead of withdrawing from situations that produce anxiety, the individual laughs at the symptoms, and instead of fighting against obsessive ideas and compulsive behaviors, or conversely, trying too hard to achieve something that remains unattainable, he or she focuses attention away from the self and toward potential meanings and values in life.[6]

Logotherapy is not practiced solely by psychotherapists. Because of its emphasis on helping the client to clarify and actualize values, Frankl believes that it provides a structure of ideas that can be used by many people who want to find direction and assume responsibility in their lives.[4]

CRITICISMS AND LIMITATIONS

A major criticism of the existential-humanistic movement is that it is not really a unified tradition but is more of a fad or slogan serving to unite— poorly—many divergent strands.[10] As a fad, it has contributed to the proliferation of many eccentric forms of encounter groups, some of whose benefits are dubious at best. Further, because of the emphasis on self-growth, this movement has been called a "cult of the self" (p. 126).[10]

It has also been criticized for lacking scientific character. Proponents of client-centered therapy have carried out quite a few research experiments in their attempts to identify the features of the therapeutic relationship that enable the client to change. Nevertheless, much of the research is seriously flawed.[11] For example, controls are often not matched to subjects in terms of their need for therapy; in some of the experiments the controls are untreated; and measures of change are often ambiguous self-report instruments. However, because the existential-humanist movement does not espouse any one technique and generally rejects scientific evaluation, it probably cannot be evaluated by prevailing scientific methods.[11]

Existential-humanism has been accused of contributing to a breakdown in the social order by its "emphasis on the freedom to choose our own rules for living" (p. 105),[11] and it has been accused of sanctioning despair and suicide.[3] But, as Dunning[3] points out, careful analysis shows that this is a life-affirming, and not a life-denying, philosophy, because the only way in which we can reconcile our eventual death is to live in a meaningful relationship with the world and ourselves.

Another criticism that has been made is that existential-humanistic psychology is often indistinguishable from classical analysis. Certainly, it shares much—philosophically and technically—with the neo-Freudian tradition, and in terms of practice, it continues in the tradition of verbal therapy that is best-suited to an articulate, highly functioning individual.

Perhaps the most relevant limitation of the existential-humanist tradition is that its view of order and disorder seems inadequate and unsatisfactory for describing the very concrete problems of daily living that are common to the chronic mentally ill persons often seen by occupational therapists.

COMMENTARY

The themes of existential-humanist psychology are relevant to occupational therapy in their provision of a perspective for understanding the value of occupation. Humanistic and existential ideas shaped the thinking of early occupational therapy leaders. Meyer and Slagle both emphasized the subjective or phenomenological aspects of performance, and the value of work and play in giving meaning to one's existence.[15]

The overriding concern of the existentialists for the individual's search for meaning in life is the backbone of the occupational therapy clinic. Yerxa, explicitly relating existentialist literature to occupational therapy, states that "authentic occupational therapy is based upon a *commitment* to the client's realization of his own particular meaning" (p. 8).[17] In this statement she captures both the phenomenological nature of disability and the actualizing potential of engaging in occupation. Clients can confront the reality of their disability in occupational therapy because they are not treated as objects with fixed limitations. Faced with the choice of doing or not doing, they are given the chance to choose their attitudes toward disability and ability, and through this choice, to find meaning in life.[17]

The idea that the client both creates and refines an understanding of self in occupational therapy is reiterated by Dunning and later by the Fidlers. In describing the occupational therapist as a humanist, Dunning notes that because "the patient must define himself, his preferences, and his skills by personal choice" (p. 476),[3] self-clarification through activity can be achieved. Likewise, the Fidlers explore the relationship of "doing" to "becoming."[5] Doing verifies one's place as a productive member of society and enables the individual to truly relate to oneself, to the physical world, and to others.

There is a growing emphasis in occupational therapy and the occupational behavior tradition on existential themes. Sharrott and Yerxa see existential thought as forming the philosophical basis of occupational therapy.[15] In the sense that the ultimate purposefulness of human occupation is the generation of meaning through personal creativity or doing, occupational therapy does serve an existential need in human beings.

The belief of occupational therapists, that patients find meaning in work, rest, and play, is inherent in the existential-humanist tradition, and makes sense only if occupational therapy is practiced within the philosophical framework of this tradition.[15] As Yerxa notes,

> Occupational therapy's use of "meaningful" and "purposeful" activity places value upon the *patient's* view of meaning. . . . In sum, the occupational therapy value system requires that our service depend upon the patient, child, or client acting in some new and personally meaningful way that moves him or her to a new state of healthfulness. (p. 27)[18]

In order to synthesize existential thought in occupational therapy with the concern for human occupation, there will have to be an interweaving of ideas concerning the biological basis of the human urge for exploration and personal mastery and ideas concerning the human experience of meaning. The volition subsystem of the Model of Human Occupation[8] is one step in this direction, as it identifies an underlying energizing component (the urge to explore and master and its biological basis in the nervous system) along with personal experience of self-ability, interests, and value.

SUMMARY

History and Purpose	European existential philosophy and phenomenological psychology are important roots of this tradition; it arose in response to mechanistic and reductionist explanations of human behavior.
View of Order	The underlying motivation for behavior is a search for self-actualization.
	Experiences and perceptions are "intentional," or shaped by one's goals.
	Authenticity, the mark of order in life, comes from an openness to experience, to oneself, and to others, and from the active pursuit of goals.
	Frankl, the founder of logotherapy, posits a "will to meaning" that leads to the discovery and choice of values, and commitment to a significant cause in life.
	For Rogers, psychosocial order is epitomized by a flexible and realistic self-image that allows for the perception and assimilation of new experiences.

View of Disorder	Neurotic anxiety is the response of the individual who cannot face the certainty of death—this anxiety manifests itself in symptomatic behavior.
	Rogers proposes that disorder occurs when the parents' love is given conditionally to the child, causing the child to reject the parts of the self-image that the parents do not seem to love.
Action Implications	Therapy emphasizes here-and-now experiences within the therapeutic relationship.
	Rogers described client-centered therapy as being the creation of an environment in which the client feels safe to re-examine self-perceptions and achieve a new self-awareness.
	Logotherapy proposes that engagement in meaningful activity helps the individual confront the existential vacuum.
	Paradoxical intention and dereflection are two techniques associated with logotherapy.
Criticisms and Limitations	The existential-humanistic movement has been considered a "cult of the self."
	It has been criticized for rejecting scientific evaluation and for using methods that are highly similar to classical analysis.
	Therapy is limited to neurotic individuals for the most part.
Commentary	Existential-humanistic themes provide a perspective for understanding the value of occupation.
	"Doing" in occupational therapy enables the individual to choose one's attitude toward one's abilities and disabilities, to relate to oneself and the world, and to find meaning in life.

TERMS AND CONCEPTS

congruence

the therapist's attempts to share honest reactions to the client with the client.

dereflection

a technique that encourages the client to direct attention to something other than the problem, to focus on other goals.

existential anxiety

feelings associated with our awareness of impending death and a sense of meaninglessness in life.

✗ *existential vacuum*

the loss of meaning in life.

✗ *intentionality*

the existential concept that one's goals influence both the choice and interpretation of one's experiences.

neurotic anxiety

feelings and behaviors that arise from denying to oneself that death is part of life.

paradoxical intention

a technique that encourages the client to do precisely what is feared.

phenomenology

a philosophy and psychology that stresses the importance of understanding human experience from the perspective of each individual, i.e., reality is subjective, not objective.

positive regard

freely given and unconditional liking for another person as an individual, without placing demands or requirements on that person's behavior.

REFERENCES

1. Becker, E. *The denial of death*. New York: Free Press, 1973.
2. Bugental, J. F. T. *Psychotherapy and process: The fundamentals of an existentalist-humanist approach*. Reading, Mass: Addison-Wesley, 1978.
3. Dunning, R. E. The occupational therapist as counselor. *American Journal of Occupational Therapy*, 1973, 27, 473–476.
4. Fabry, J. B. Logotherapy in action: An overview. In J. B. Fabry, R. P. Bueka, & W. S. Sahakian (Eds.), *Logotherapy in action*. New York: Jason Aronson, 1979.
5. Fidler, G. S., & Fidler, J. W. Doing and becoming: Purposeful action and self-actualization. *American Journal of Occupational Therapy*, 1978, 32, 305–310.
6. Frankl, V. E. *The doctor and the soul*. New York: Alfred Knopf, 1972.

7. Frankl, V. E. *Psychotherapy and existential papers on logotherapy*. New York: Square Press, 1967.
8. Kielhofner, G., & Burke, J. P. A model of human occupation. *American Journal of Occupational Therapy*, 1980, *34*, 572–581.
9. Meador, B. D., & Rogers, C. R. Person-centered therapy. In R. J. Corsini (Ed.), *Current psychotherapies* (2nd ed.). Itasca, Ill.: Peacock, 1979.
10. Misiak, H., & Sexton, V. S. *Phenomenological, existential, and humanistic psychologies: A historical survey*. New York: Grune & Stratton, 1973.
11. Prochaska, J. O. *Systems of psychotherapy: A transtheoretical analysis*. Homewood, Ill.: Dorsey, 1979.
12. Rogers, C. R. *Client-centered therapy*. Boston: Houghton Mifflin, 1961.
13. Sahakian, W. S. Logotherapy—For whom? In J. B. Fabry, R. P. Bueka, & W. S. Sahakian (Eds.), *Logotherapy in action*. New York: Jason Aronson, 1979.
14. Shaffer, J. B. P. *Humanistic psychology*. Englewood Cliffs, N.J.: Prentice-Hall, 1978.
15. Sharrott, G. W., & Yerxa, E. J. *Existentialism as the philosophical base of occupational therapy, Parts I and II*. Unpublished paper, Department of Occupational Therapy, University of Southern California, 1982.
16. Ungersma, A. J. *The search for meaning*. Philadelphia: Westminster Press, 1961.
17. Yerxa, E. J. Authentic occupational therapy. *American Journal of Occupational Therapy*, 1967, *21*, 1–9.
18. Yerxa, E. J. The philosophical base of occupational therapy. In *Occupational Therapy—2001*. Rockville, Md.: American Occupational Therapy Assoc., 1979.

ADDITIONAL READINGS

Bugental, J. F. T. (Ed.). *Challenges of humanistic psychology*. New York: McGraw-Hill, 1967.
Ellul, J. [*The technological society*.] (J. Wilkinson, trans.). New York: Knopf, 1964.
Frankl, V. E. *The unheard cry for meaning*. New York: Simon & Schuster, 1978.
Koestembaum, P. *The new image of the person*. Westport, Conn.: Greenwood Press, 1978.
Rogers, C. R. *On becoming a person*. Boston: Houghton Mifflin, 1961.
Tillich, P. *The courage to be*. New Haven: Yale Press, 1952.

5

Behavioral Approaches

Behavioral approaches represent a substantial body of knowledge and techniques developed to treat a wide range of problems. While there are several focuses within the behavioral tradition, they all share a concern for the use of research-supported methods; a view of behavior as being strongly influenced by reinforcing conditions; and a belief that changes in behavior precede changes in thought, attitude, and emotion. Proponents of behavioral approaches argue that they provide the most effective and efficient way to change overt behavior and eventually to have an impact on cognition and affect.[2]

Behavioral techniques have developed from experimental research on principles of reinforcement (learning principles). Both theory and practice are rigorously grounded in quantitative animal and human research. Careful attention is given to operationally (behaviorally) defining target behaviors for treatment, quantifying behavior, and measuring treatment outcomes. This foundation in research supports behaviorists' confidence in the effectiveness and efficiency of their techniques.

The behavioral approach, regardless of the "brand" practiced, typically focuses on outward behavior, rather than inner psychological processes, and views adaptive and maladaptive behaviors as learned through reinforcement. However, more recently, some behavioral theorists and practitioners have become concerned with the relationship between cognitive processes and behavioral changes.[5]

At its inception, this approach, being unique among therapies for psychosocial dysfunction, created excitement and greatly increased clinical research. On the other hand, it stirred controversy and distrust among adherents of more traditional approaches that emphasized the emotional disorder underlying observable behavior and the therapeutic relationship.

The use of behavioral techniques has been investigated with many different problematic behaviors. Its clinical applications are myriad, ranging from people with mild phobias to psychotic children and adults needing to learn skills. Behaviorists do not consider psychiatric diagnoses to be useful guides for treatment. Any maladaptive behavior believed to be amenable to relearning is accepted by behaviorists as a legitimate target for treatment.

HISTORY AND PURPOSE

Since the beginning of time, people have "commonsensically" used certain behavioral principles learned from everyday experiences. However, behaviorism as an identifiable body of knowledge with scientific hypothesis testing and statement of lawful relationships is commonly traced back to Pavlov, a turn of the century Russian physiologist.

The methods of the behavioral tradition are modeled on the physical sciences (e.g., chemistry) in the interest of achieving similarly precise scientific techniques. Behaviorists reduce human behaviors to their smallest observable units in an effort to understand their characteristics and functions. Just as chemists analyze atoms and molecules to understand complex chemical reactions, behaviorists study the units of response and stimulus that eventually add up to complex individual and social behaviors.[10] Wolpe[16] defines a response simply as "a behavioral event" and a stimulus as "the antecedent of a response" (p. 14). Complex behavior is accordingly seen as the simultaneous interaction of many responses, each of which becomes the stimulus for future events.[16] As one behaviorist notes, learning has occurred

> . . . if a response has been evoked in temporal contiguity with a given sensory stimulus and it is subsequently found that the stimulus can evoke the response although it could not have done so before. If the stimulus could have evoked the response before but subsequently evokes it more strongly, then, too, learning may be said to have occurred. (p. 260)[15]

Thus, behaviorists seek to analyze and understand complex human actions through the study of component parts and their causal relations. Two major traditions have evolved to make up the behavioral approach: classical and operant conditioning.

Classical Conditioning

Pavlov was interested in the process by which a new stimulus would come to elicit the response previously associated with another stimulus. The new stimulus is referred to as a conditioned stimulus. Unconditioned stimuli are typically connected to smooth muscle functioning such as glandular operations. Pavlov found that dogs salivated (an unconditioned response) at the sight of food. By pairing the unconditioned stimulus of food with another stimulus such as the sound of a bell, the latter eventually elicited salivation—now a conditioned response—without the presence of food. The sound of the bell, then, became a conditioned stimulus.[10] Pavlov therefore concluded that if two stimuli were repeatedly and simultaneously presented, the weaker, secondary stimulus came to elicit the same response that only the stronger (unconditioned) stimulus previously elicited alone. This model is called Pavlovian or classical conditioning.

A significant development out of the classical conditioning model is counterconditioning. In this process, a subject learns a fear-inhibiting response such as calmness. The connection between fear (or anxiety) and the stimulus that produces fear is weakened as the subject experiences the incompatible response (calmness) in the presence of the stimulus.[16] In 1958, Wolpe presented the principle that describes how counterconditioning occurs.[17] Pavlov, Wolpe, and others developed one tradition within behaviorism based on the original classical conditioning model and extended this in the counterconditioning model to form the tradition of "behavior therapy."

Operant Conditioning

The works of Thorndike and Skinner characterize the other major tradition within behaviorism. Their similar observations that behavior was controlled by consequences[7] led to the development of a technology based on operant methods. The model derived from their works is called instrumental, operant, or Skinnerian conditioning.

Skinner's work in the 1930s was built on the simple principle that all responses had consequences.[10] He demonstrated that by manipulating consequences, one could control the occurrence of particular behaviors. For example, if one provided food pellets to hungry rats when they pressed a lever, their lever-pressing behavior increased. The behavior that increased was said to have been positively reinforced. Negative reinforcement works on the principle that unpleasant consequences (e.g., shock) could increase frequency of avoidance or escape behaviors. The name operant conditioning was applied because the organism's response (for example, lever pressing) *operated* on the environment to achieve the desired effect.[10] Such early observations led to experiments seeking ways to establish, eliminate, increase, or decrease the frequency of behaviors. A science of positive and negative reinforcement with delineation of schedules of reinforcement was thus developed.

Further Developments

In the 1950s, Wolpe began to apply behavioral methods to the treatment of neurotic patients. He developed an approach called reciprocal inhibition through systematic desensitization.[17] He believed neurotic behavior was learned in the presence of fear-producing stimuli, and he conceptualized treatment as the reversal of this learning.[6] In other words, the patient needed to learn to produce relaxed, nonneurotic behavior in the presence of the original stimuli. To do this, Wolpe used progressive relaxation techniques, assertion training, and the operant conditioning methods of positive and negative reinforcement and extinction.[16]

Bandura represents another significant direction of behavior theory, research, and practice: social learning theory. He studied the impact of modeling and other vicarious learning processes, rather than the direct effects of reinforcement.[1]

Throughout this discussion, the behavioral tradition will be presented as a whole. However, a distinction is sometimes made between two broad focuses of the behavioral tradition: behavior modification and behavior therapy. Whenever someone exerts a degree of control over others, as in such varied interpersonal situations as the classroom, advertising, and political campaigns, behavior influence has occurred. Behavior modification is a special type of behavior influence based on the Skinnerian principle that persons' behaviors are influenced by consequences.[13] Behavior modification is mainly an operant approach that has developed in inpatient institutional settings, especially from work with mentally retarded and severely mentally ill patients. Principles of positive and negative reinforcement, punishment and extinction; techniques of shaping, chaining, fading, and prompting; and programs such as the token economy are characteristic of a behavior modification approach.[6]

Some writers speak of behavior therapy as a type of behavior modification used in a one-to-one clinical relationship.[13] Others see behavior therapy as the behavioral treatment of neurotic behavior developed in outpatient settings and not as a subset of behavior modification. In it, the classical conditioning model is more prevalent. This is evidenced by the concern for counterconditioning anxiety or the relearning of more adaptive emotional responses and fear reduction techniques.[6] While behavior modification and behavior therapy are separate branches of behavioral treatment, their uses of models and techniques overlap.

VIEW OF ORDER

The view of order in behaviorism incorporates several interrelated themes. It is heavily influenced by the fact that behaviorists have incorporated the world view of the physical sciences into their understanding of human order. Consequently, the themes relating to order are: (1) humans, like machines, are causally and environmentally determined entities; (2) humans are hedonistic, drive-centered beings; and (3) humans are homeostatic and moved by cause-and-effect forces. From this foundation, other themes emerge.

The fundamental operating principle in human behavior is thought to be a process of seeking a state of nontension (homeostasis). From a purist behavioral viewpoint, tension arises from disruptions in tissue states (e.g., hunger). Behavior is oriented to reducing these tensions (e.g., by obtaining and consuming food). In this sense, all behavior is goal-oriented (i.e., oriented to achieving a reduction in tension), and stimuli are viewed in terms of their relevance to goals programmed into the organism. Consequences of behavior that reduce tension reinforce and shape behavior. For example, a rat comes to press a lever because this action leads to getting food (a goal-oriented behavior) which when consumed reduces the tension of hunger. These underlying tensions are also referred to as drives.

The concept of drives arising from disturbances of homeostasis is central to early behaviorist thought. It is from the underlying drives that the stimuli and consequent behavior derive their relevance to the organism's behavior. Stimuli exist and have meaning to the organism only as they complement drive states. While more recent thought and practice in behaviorism is not as strictly bound to the concept of drives, the idea of the human being as a goal-oriented, tension-reducing organism still tends to permeate behaviorist thinking. Related to drive theory is the assumption that the motivation for human behavior is basically hedonistic or pleasure-seeking in nature; that is, humans act to satisfy their drives, avoid discomforts, and attain the pleasure associated with tension-reduction. In addition, behaviorist thought stresses the degree to which humans are shaped by their environments, because environmental conditions will either allow or prevent the organism's tension-reduction.

In behaviorism, ordered behavior is a function of the causal laws that determine how environmental stimuli and consequences influence behavior. These laws or principles seek to explain how the environment shapes and determines behavior, and they are equally applicable to the explanation of disorder and order. The distinction between order and disorder, therefore, does not lie in how behavior is acquired, but in the eventual success of this behavior in meeting the organism's needs and in its social acceptability.

While a large number of these causal laws exist describing how behavior is influenced by the environment, only two will be described here to illustrate the general nature of these laws. The first is the law of intermittent reinforcement. It has been found that the timing of reinforcement presentation is one of the most important factors in the effectiveness of a reinforcer's influence on behavior. Continuous reinforcement exists when every behavioral response is reinforced; this method is generally used when the researcher seeks to establish a new behavior. Intermittent reinforcement occurs when not every behavior is reinforced; reinforcement may be random or on some schedule, such as every second or third response. The law of intermittent

73

reinforcement states that behavior that is reinforced periodically (intermittently) rather than constantly is less likely to subside or be extinguished once reinforcement is withdrawn.[7]

Reciprocal inhibition is another causal law; this refers to a situation in which two incompatible responses are elicited by the same stimulus, leading to the extinction of one of the responses. For instance, "if a response inhibiting anxiety can be made to occur in the presence of anxiety-evoking stimuli, it will weaken the bond between these stimuli and the anxiety" (p. 17).[16] This principle is the most frequently used to inhibit anxiety or fear responses in the treatment of neurotic behavior with methods of counterconditioning.

Such laws as intermittent reinforcement and reciprocal inhibition describe the many ways in which stimuli and consequences (reinforcers) influence behavior. Together these principles constitute a network of lawful relations that describe how human behavior is ordered.

Most of these principles have been generated from experimental situations and, therefore, are more exact than the way such principles operate in everyday life. For example, the principle of intermittent reinforcement refers to how the timing of reinforcement affects behavior in the laboratory, yet its application is generalized to all human situations. Intermittent reinforcement, like all behavioral principles, is assumed to be one of the causal laws operating in human life. Importantly, the view of order in behaviorism comes from laboratory experiments rather than from naturalistic observation of human beings in their everyday settings.

As previously noted, the theme of environmental determination is implicit in this view of human behavior as influenced by cause-and-effect laws. Humans are viewed as passive respondents to events, having learned, or having been shaped, conditioned, or molded by environmental events. As Skinner, a radical behaviorist, argues, human freedom is simply an illusion, a form of wishful thinking.[12] No mention is made of humans creating their experiences, originating events, or acting out of a natural desire simply to act. Goldstein states this view straightforwardly:

> Determinism, the concept that every behavior is completely determined by antecedent factors, is the most basic concept relative to the development or change of personality. Behavior therapists absolutely deny the concept of free will in that sense that one ever behaves in a way which is not contingent upon antecedent events. (p. 219)[6]

Classically, little attention has been given to inner processes, although some behaviorists have more recently acknowledged the role of cognition and blended their practice with cognitive restructuring methods. This is an important shift

74

to the recognition of the influence of cognitive processes, attitudes, and thoughts on behavior.[6]

Finally, in the behavioral tradition order is recognizable by its adaptive consequences which:

> take the form of progress toward the satisfaction of a need . . . or the avoidance of possible damage or deprivation. . . . All this may be summarized by saying that behavior is adaptive to the extent that it is "worth while." (p. 32)[17]

A person in a state of order, then, is one who satisfies basic drives in a socially acceptable fashion while reacting to environmental influences.

VIEW OF DISORDER

The behaviorist views disorder not in terms of inner conflicts and diagnoses, but rather as maladaptive behaviors resulting from faulty learning. That is to say, the disordered individual was reinforced or conditioned to act in ways that did not meet the individual's needs or which were not socially acceptable. Faulty learning may refer either to failure to acquire a particular skill or to acquisition of a socially disruptive behavior. Socially disruptive behavior may be self-satisfying but shows little regard for others' needs and hampers others' adaptive performance. In this case, the behavior will eventually interfere with the subject's adaptation. In other cases, the appropriate behavioral cues (stimuli) may not have been learned, so that an individual expresses a certain skilled behavior at inappropriate times or in inappropriate settings.

Examples of the range of behaviors addressed by the behaviorist help to clarify the scope of disorders dealt with and the behavioral approach to classifying disorders as either the presence of undesirable behaviors or the absence of desired behaviors. For instance, behavior modification techniques are used with retarded persons to counteract unwanted behaviors such as self-abuse, head banging, masturbation, undressing, kicking, screaming, and biting; to teach new behaviors such as the self-help skills of dressing, showering, and speech; to treat "odd behaviors" such as tics and mutism; and to treat substance abuse behavior.[10] Behavior therapy is used to reduce anxiety responses and phobias; to treat learned maladaptive habits such as nail biting and tantrums; and to correct the maladaptive habits of schizophrenic and psychopathic people. As the examples illustrate, behaviorally oriented practitioners rely on commonsense definitions of what is inappropriate. They explain all these "disorders" as products of faulty learning, meaning that in the past, behaviors were not appropriately paired with stimuli and reinforced.

ACTION IMPLICATIONS

Defining disorder in terms of outward behavioral responses yields a treatment focus on changing behaviors and modifying the observable, measurable manifestations of emotional responses associated with objects and events. The emphasis on the overriding role of environmental impact on the person is reflected in the goals of therapy and in the role of the behavioral therapist.

The general goal of behavioral treatment is to provide environments that promote learning or relearning for a person in whom the learning of effective behavior previously never took place or was lost. Through the treatment process, the patient is not made to feel ill or symptomatic, but simply is viewed as the recipient of faulty learning. This puts the responsibility on the therapist to treat the patient effectively as measured by target behavior changes or to revise the treatment program. When therapy does not work, the therapist admits personal inability to devise effective behavior change strategies, rather than blaming issues such as patient resistance.

Behavioral treatment is generally characterized by two types of evaluation. First, the therapist does an analysis of the problematic behavior and its antecedent and contingent surrounding events (stimuli and reinforcing behavior).[2] Second, the effectiveness of treatment techniques and programs is evaluated.

In the patient evaluation phase of treatment, the therapist seeks to determine what typically happens before and after those behaviors targeted for treatment. This may involve a history-taking interview, recording of baseline data of observed behaviors, and/or administration of a standard test. The goal is to identify maladaptive behaviors ("target behaviors") and the set of circumstances in which they occur. This careful analysis is performed for the purpose of understanding the stimulus-response relationships that support the behaviors.

The next phase of treatment involves continued information gathering, formation of hypotheses about the target behaviors (i.e., how they came about and how they can be changed), and further development of the cooperative working relationship with the identified patient or patient representative (as in the case of a child or severely cognitively impaired patient). This phase has been referred to as a relationship-building phase of therapy and involves development of a cooperative working relationship between the therapist and patient, leading to the design of a treatment program.[6]

Treatment methods for establishing new behaviors, both simple and complex, include shaping by successive approximation, chaining, prompting, fading, modeling, role playing, and behavioral rehearsal. *Shaping by successive approximation* is an operant method that uses reinforcement of incremental steps, building from the absence of the desired behavior to its free expression. In this process, behavior is shaped by reinforcing closer and more exact expressions of the final preferred performance.[10] *Chaining* is another operant technique in which a series of related simple behaviors are reinforced to establish a larger more complex behavioral unit (chain). These chains are typically taught in reverse order. For example, with dressing, all but the last event—putting shoes on—will be performed for the person. The subject will be taught the last step first, since it is most reinforcing for the subject to have completed a complex behavior. The subject then continues learning in this "backward" sequence until the entire chain of behaviors called dressing is mastered.[7] *Prompting* involves simply directing the subject's attention to the task. This may be done by physically guiding the learner to perform a given behavior or through more subtle use of verbal cues or signals. *Fading* refers to the gradual cessation of these prompts so that natural, more subtle elements in the environment will come to evoke appropriate behavior without the learner's reliance on artificial prompts.[7] *Modeling* involves demonstrating the desired behavior for the learner and can communicate the subtle or expressive qualities of complex behavior.[8] In *role playing*, the person practices a role he or she normally does not perform without the risks of being in a "real life" situation.[4] *Behavioral rehearsal* combines modeling techniques with role playing.[8,9] In these techniques, positive and negative reinforcement and stimulus control (which involves manipulation of antecedents of behavior to effect the likelihood of the behavioral event's occurring) are used to increase the frequency of desirable behavior.[7]

To decrease undesirable behaviors, the techniques of punishment, response cost, time out, extinction, and satiation are used. *Punishment* involves either presenting an aversive stimulus, removing a positive reinforcer, or presenting a neutral stimulus to decrease or stop the frequency of a particular behavior.[7] It is properly used to decrease immediately dangerous behavior or to control behaviors that cannot be modified by manipulating cues or consequences. *Response cost* is a type of punishment in which known reinforcers are taken away when undesirable behavior is expressed. In *time out*, the subject is removed from the setting in which he or she might receive reinforcers. Thus, it is time out from reinforcement. Time out is used when the attention that is given to disruptive behaviors may be unintentionally serving as a positive reinforcement. *Extinction* involves withdrawing the reinforcement to eliminate a behavior. *Satiation* involves continuous reinforcement over a brief time period so that the subject becomes tired of responding and the reinforcer becomes less powerful as it becomes readily accessible.[7]

Behavioral techniques are used with individuals, in group settings such as in assertion training groups, and as an integral part of the structure of ward culture, as in token economies.

CRITICISMS AND LIMITATIONS

Three main criticisms of behaviorism found in the literature are: (1) the inadequacy of the behavioral approach on the issue of motivation; (2) the limitations of the reductionist nature of the approach; and (3) the concerns over ethical issues in the control of behavior.

Florey[3] and White[14] have pointed out the inadequacy of behaviorism for explaining much spontaneous human behavior. The behaviorist approach refers solely to extrinsic sources of motivation in which behavior occurs because it serves a goal outside itself (e.g., eating to reduce hunger). However, not all behavior occurs because of such extrinsic rewards or reinforcements. There is a class of spontaneously occurring, creative, initiative actions which are performed for the simple pleasure of action itself, for having an impact on one's surroundings, and for the feelings of competence accrued from having effects on the environment. Such behavior is said to be intrinsically motivated (i.e., the motive lies within the behavior itself). In addition, these writers reject the idea that all behavior is tension-reducing.[3,14] White postulates a tension-seeking drive for competence. This urge for competence leads the organism to act for action itself or for the pleasure of being a cause or having competence. Skinner[11] rebuts the notion of intrinsic motivation, claiming that the scientific approach to the study of behavior cannot admit to the "self as a true originator or initiator of action" (p. 225).

A criticism of radical behaviorism is the inadequacy of its scientific methods for the study of complex human behavior. Based on the methods of physical science, behaviorists practice reductionism, analyzing the causal relationships of behavioral components, then providing treatment with the expectation that these remediated components when reassembled will yield functional, adaptive performance and a healthy, ordered individual. Critics of this approach point out that human behavior is a gestalt that must be studied in a more holistic fashion.[14]

Thus, both of these criticisms argue that the behaviorist approach oversimplifies the explanation of human behavior. However, the problem may not be one of simplicity versus complexity but rather of adequacy. In its view of motivation and its reductionistic approach, behavioral theory is incomplete and, therefore, inadequate for fully understanding behavior.

A third issue is the ethical considerations that arise over treatment and research aimed at behavior control, especially with involuntarily confined patients. These concerns are typically countered by behaviorists who state that *all* therapy involves some control of behavior and that people control each other daily. Behaviorists argue that they are simply more straightforward and systematic in addressing the issue of manipulation. Other rebuttals suggest that the behavioral treatment is really offering a person more control of his or her life by introducing greater access to tools of self-control.[10,13]

Another criticism frequently voiced by practitioners from other theoretical orientations is that behavioral techniques effect only a superficial change and that underlying cognitive and affective symptoms will reappear in new contexts. Still others accept the evidence of behavioral changes but believe that cognitive mediating processes, and not simply the behavioral techniques, are the reason changes occur in "behavioral treatment." This criticism has led to extensions of behavioral theory and methods to include concerns with cognition. While cognitive approaches grew out of some behaviorists' works, they differ significantly and, thus, are treated in the following chapter.

Criticisms of behaviorism abound, and their validity is at times difficult to discern. The charge of inadequacy of the behavioral view of motivation seems to be a reasonable concern. Daily experience provides numerous examples of activities that are difficult if not impossible to explain in terms of behavioral theory (e.g., those who enjoy the sport of rock climbing, a highly risky venture to physical integrity). The charge of reductionism appears to be a debate of magnitude. Skinner argues that what is lost when one focuses on components is minor,[11] while critics see the loss of perspective as significant. Ethical debates must always be kept in the fore, reminding all who work in the helping professions to be cognizant not only of the direct impact of treatment intervention, but also of the possibility of the incidental impact of therapy on patients and the implications of whether one covertly or overtly attempts to change people. Finally, the practical concerns of whether the most important, in depth, lasting, and meaningful changes are being effected in patients, as well as teasing out the exact reasons for behavior change, are the most difficult to judge and remain to be demonstrated.

COMMENTARY

Decisions about the value and compatibility of behaviorism with occupational therapy must be considered from the perspective of whether behaviorism matches the goals and processes of the field. Occupational therapy has as a fundamental theoretical concept a belief in the naturally motivating quality of activity. Initially, this appears incompatible with the behavorist premise that behavior is extrinsically motivated. However, a more adequate perspective for the occupational therapist is to recognize that both extrinsic and intrinsic motives for behavior exist. In that sense, occupational therapy approaches that stress activity for its own sake and behavioral approaches that change behavior through reinforcement can be seen as complementary. Similarly, the use of some behavioral technology adjunctively with occupational therapy can supplement treatment.

Based on the occupational therapy tradition, theory, and practice, it is not the role of the therapist to participate in the development of a purely behavioristic overall treatment program or to design an occupational therapy program based on behavioral principles. However, a dilemma sometimes arises for occupational therapists who find themselves working within a total treatment milieu (e.g., a ward or total program) that is based on behavioral principles. Here the therapist must ask how the occupational therapy approach can fit into such a program. In such a situation, the therapist should recognize the utility of building a program that uses extrinsic rewards to alter behavior, while developing an occupational therapy approach that provides activities that are motivating because of their intrinsic interest and meaning. Even within a predominantly behavioral approach, it is important to recognize that persons are motivated by and do some activities simply because they provide stimulation and a feeling of competence. Thus, the occupational therapy program can add balance to the overall program.

This is not to suggest that techniques developed by behaviorists or which reflect behaviorist principles never enter into the occupational therapy process. There are really two points to consider. First, a number of techniques have been developed by behaviorists that neither solely reflect nor strictly originate from behavioral principles. Such processes as modeling, relaxation techniques, role playing, and giving praise are techniques that behaviorists write about, use, and have refined in practice. However, these methods are not exclusively behavioral techniques. Other theoretical writers and practitioners, including occupational therapists using nonbehaviorist orientations have described and used similar techniques. For instance, relaxation techniques help to manage anxiety and may thus be used to provide clients with a self-help tool to calm themselves and maximize the benefits of involvement in occupational therapy. In similar ways occupational therapists use role playing to enhance occupational therapy activities. Thus, the therapist will undoubtedly find himself or herself using techniques that have been used by behaviorists. However, this does not mean the therapist is using a behavioral approach.

Second, there are instances when occupational therapists will find it compatible to use techniques based on behavioral principles in concert with their own approach. For instance, an adolescent boy with behavioral problems may be in the woodshop to explore, to pursue interests, and to develop competence. These are all processes that are defined by a different (nonbehavioral) theoretical tradition of promoting competence and health. That same adolescent may be told that if he acts out while in the woodshop, he will experience certain negative consequences. Here, the healthy behavior (i.e., woodworking) is motivated through the intrinsic motives of interest and challenge, while the unhealthy behavior is controlled by extrinsic motives (the threat of punishment). An inappropriate use of behavioral techniques in this case would be to reward the adolescent for working in the woodshop.

It is worth noting additionally that the behavioral approach to treatment is more than its learning-based techniques. Thus, other dimensions of behaviorism may have relevance for occupational therapists. Careful determination of target behaviors, clear specification of treatment procedures through clear goal setting and progress measures, and reliance on objective, verifiable data to evaluate treatment outcomes are valuable for any approach to treatment and, indeed, are advocated by other traditions as well.

Behaviorists and occupational therapists focus on different aspects of human behavior (i.e., intrinsically versus extrinsically motivated behavior). Complex psychosocial problems typically require the efforts and techniques available through collaboration of disciplines. An important contribution of the occupational therapist to overall program design is to point out the necessity of a balanced approach in which both intrinsic and extrinsic motives for behavior are recognized and nourished.

SUMMARY

History and Purpose	Behaviorism is a research- and learning theory-based science of behavior with a systematic approach to analyzing and treating observable behaviors, rather than inner psychological processes. Any maladaptive behavior amenable to relearning is considered treatable by behaviorists.
	It is based on models of the physical sciences, and its origin is commonly traced back to the work of Pavlov and his model of classical conditioning. The operant conditioning model associated with Skinner, counterconditioning associated with Wolpe, and social learning theories of Bandura are further significant developments.
	Two broad areas within behaviorism are behavior therapy, based on classical conditioning, and behavior modification, based on an operant model.

View of Order	Behaviorists tend to view people reductionistically, as machine-like, moved by cause-and-effect forces, and as being homeostatic in nature. Thus, people are seen as goal oriented, seeking tension reduction, and acting hedonistically.
	Human actions are believed to be environmentally determined, that is, shaped by the environment to the degree that all behavior is understood as the result of laws of conditioning and reinforcement and as dependent on environmental cues for its enactment.
	Numerous principles describe how order comes about. These include reinforcement schedules and reciprocal inhibition, among others.
	A person in a state of order is one who satisfies basic drives while reacting to environmental influences.
View of Disorder	Disorder is viewed as the result of faulty learning. Disordered overt behavior, not inner processes, is the object of behavioral treatment interventions.
Action Implications	Behavior theory and research have been translated into numerous systematic principles and techniques for changing outward behavior. The goal of behavioral treatment is, then, to provide environments that promote learning or relearning. The evaluation phase is well-developed, characterized by (1) careful gathering of data on behavior and the events that support it and (2) evaluation of treatment techniques and program effectiveness.
	There are specific techniques to establish new behaviors, increase the frequency of desired behaviors, and decrease the frequency of undesired behaviors.

Criticisms and Limitations	Behaviorism has been criticized for its exclusively extrinsic view of motivation, for its narrow reductionistic approach, and for ethical concerns with behavior control. Additionally, nonbehavioral clinicians charge that the changes in behavior are superficial. Those who may be considered cognitive-behavioral in orientation suggest that the behavior changes occur, but some cognitive process is really influencing the change.
Commentary	Occupational therapy uses techniques which are similar to those discussed in behavioral literature. Some of these include modeling, role playing, relaxation techniques, and giving praise. However, these do not belong exclusively to behaviorism. The fundamental importance of intrinsic motivation to the occupational therapy process is the key principle to keep in mind. Occupational therapy per se does not rely on deliberate, planned use of extrinsic rewards.

TERMS AND CONCEPTS

behavior modification	a major branch of behaviorism based on the Skinnerian principle that behaviors are influenced by consequences. It is mainly an operant approach.
behavior therapy	a major branch of behaviorism associated with the behavioral treatment of neurotic behavior. In it, the classical conditioning model is more prevalent.
behavioral rehearsal	a combination of modeling techniques with role playing used to teach new, complex behaviors.
chaining	an operant technique in which a series of related simple behaviors are reinforced to establish a larger more complex unit (chain). These chains are typically taught in reverse order.
classical conditioning	the early behavioral model based on Pavlov's studies. The basic law of this model states that a previously neutral event will come to elicit the same response as an event that naturally elicits that response when the two events are repeatedly paired.

counterconditioning	a further development after classical conditioning based on the principle of reciprocal inhibition explained by Wolpe. This is a process in which the subject learns a fear-inhibiting response so that the connection between fear and the stimulus object producing fear is weakened as the subject experiences the incompatible response in the presence of the stimulus.
environmental determinism	a basic behaviorist belief that humans passively respond to and are shaped by the environment.
extinction	a technique that involves withdrawing the reinforcement to eliminate a behavior.
fading	the gradual cessation of prompts so that natural, more subtle elements in the environment will come to evoke appropriate behavior without the learner's reliance on artificial prompts.
faulty learning	occurs when the individual is reinforced or conditioned to act in ways that do not meet the individual's needs or are not socially acceptable.
modeling	demonstrating desired behavior for the learner in order to communicate the subtle or expressive qualities of complex behavior.
operant conditioning	a behaviorist model characterized in the writings of Skinner which state that all responses have consequences and behavior is controlled by these. Thus, by manipulating the consequences, one could control the occurrence of particular behavior. Also called Skinnerian and instrumental conditioning.
prompting	involves simply directing the subject's attention to a task. This may be done by physically guiding the learner to perform a given behavior or through more subtle use of verbal cues or signals.
punishment	involves either presenting an aversive stimulus, removing a positive reinforcer, or presenting a neutral stimulus to decrease or stop the frequency of a particular behavior.

reciprocal inhibition   eliciting two incompatible responses leading to the extinction of one of the responses. This principle is the most frequently used to inhibit anxiety or fear responses in the treatment of neurotic behavior using methods of counterconditioning.

reinforcer   a stimulus which, when contingent on an operant response, will maintain or enhance the likelihood of that operant response occurring.

response   one of two basic units of behavioral study. A response is the behavioral event that follows a stimulus. The stimulus and response together constitute the next larger unit of behavioral study.

response cost   a type of punishment in which known reinforcers are taken away when undesirable behavior is expressed.

role playing   a technique to establish new behaviors that requires that the client practice a role in the treatment setting which he or she normally does not perform, without the risks of being in a "real life" situation.

satiation   a technique to decrease undesirable behaviors that involves continuous reinforcement over a brief time period so that the subject becomes tired of responding and the reinforcer becomes less powerful as it becomes readily accessible.

schedules of reinforcement   the timing of reinforcement presentation. This has an important influence on the effectiveness of the reinforcement.

social learning theory   an area of behavioral study associated with Bandura in which the impact of modeling and other vicarious learning processes are studied rather than the direct effects of reinforcement.

shaping by successive approximation   an operant method that uses reinforcement of incremental steps along a continuum, building from the absence of the desired behavior to its expression. Behavior is viewed as being shaped by the process of reinforcing closer and more exact expressions of the final preferred performance.

stimulus	one of two basic units of behavioral study. A stimulus is the event that precedes a response. The stimulus and response together constitute the next larger unit of behavioral study.
tension reduction	an underlying belief of behaviorists that the human organism acts to decrease tension arising from disruption of tissue states (e.g., hunger). Behavior is believed to occur for the purpose of relieving such tension.
time out	a technique for decreasing undesirable behaviors in which the subject is removed from the setting in which he or she might receive reinforcers.

REFERENCES

1. Bandura, A. *Principles of behavior modification*. New York: Holt, Rinehart & Winston, 1969.
2. Freedman, A. M., Kaplan, H. I., & Sadock, B. J. *Modern synopsis of comprehensive textbook of psychiatry* (2nd ed.). Baltimore: Williams & Wilkins, 1976.
3. Florey, L. L. Intrinsic motivation: The dynamics of occupational therapy. *American Journal of Occupational Therapy*, 1969, *23*, 319–322.
4. Flowers, J. V. Simulation and role playing methods. In F. H. Kanfer & A. P. Goldstein (Eds.), *Helping people change*. New York: Pergamon, 1975.
5. Goldfried, M. R., & Goldfried, A. P. Cognitive change methods. In F. H. Kanfer & A. P. Goldstein (Eds.), *Helping people change*. New York: Pergamon, 1975.
6. Goldstein, A. Behavior therapy. In R. Corsini (Ed.), *Current psychotherapies*. Itasca, Ill.: F. E. Peacock Publishers, 1973.
7. Karoly, P. Operant methods. In F. H. Kanfer & A. P. Goldstein (Eds.), *Helping people change*. New York: Pergamon, 1975.
8. Liberman, R. P., King, L. W., DeRisi, W. J., & McCann, M. *Personal effectiveness: Guiding people to assert themselves and improve their social skills*. Champaign, Ill.: Research Press, 1975.
9. Marlatt, G. A., & Perry, M. H. Modeling methods. In F. H. Kanfer & A. P. Goldstein (Eds.), *Helping people change*. New York: Pergamon, 1975.
10. Schaefer, H. H., & Martin, P. L. *Behavior therapy* (2nd ed.). New York: McGraw-Hill, 1975.

11. Skinner, B. F. *About behaviorism*. New York: Alfred A. Knopf, 1974.
12. Skinner, B. F. *Beyond freedom and dignity*. New York: Alfred A. Knopf, 1971.
13. Stolz, S. B., Wienckowski, L. A., & Brown, B. S. Behavior modification: A perspective on critical issues. *American Psychologist*, 1975, *30*, 1027–1947.
14. White, R. W. The urge towards competence. *American Journal of Occupational Therapy*, 1971, *25*, 271–274.
15. Wolpe, J. Experimental neuroses as learned behaviour. *British Journal of Psychology*, 1952, *43*, 243–268.
16. Wolpe, J. *The practice of behavior therapy* (2nd ed.). Oxford: Pergamon, 1973.
17. Wolpe, J. *Psychotherapy by reciprocal inhibition*. Stanford, Calif.: Stanford University Press, 1958.

ADDITIONAL READINGS

Buckholdt, D. R., & Gubrium, J. F. *Caretakers: Treating emotionally disturbed children*. Beverly Hills, Calif.: Sage, 1979.

Corsini, R., & Contributors. *Current psychotherapies* (2nd ed.). Itasca, Ill.: F. E. Peacock Publishers, 1979.

Kanfer, F. H., & Goldstein, A. P. (Eds.). *Helping people change*. New York: Pergamon, 1975.

Lange, A. J., & Jakubowski, P. *Responsible assertive behavior: Cognitive/behavioral procedures for trainees*. Champaign, Ill.: Research Press, 1976.

Mosey, A. C. *Three frames of reference for mental health*. Thorofare, N. J.: Charles B. Slack, 1971.

6

Cognitive Approaches to Therapy

The cognitive approaches to therapy, sometimes called semantic therapies, are relatively new and represent a collection of varied techniques from divergent traditions. Yet, they all share concern for the impact that cognitive functions such as beliefs, attributions, assumptions, and expectations have on affect and behavior. In addition, this concern is combined with the use of research-based techniques of behaviorism.[6] In theory, these approaches may be viewed as existing on a continuum from purely cognitive to a combination of cognitive-behavioral treatment; however the exact boundaries of this body of knowledge are not agreed upon. While there are some common concerns shared by cognitive therapists, the field is still in the process of definition and seeking to prove its effectiveness and gain respectability.

While some theorists see cognitive therapy as a recent model in the behavioral tradition,[14] there are others who consider cognitive therapy to be totally distinct.[7] A crucial difference between cognitive and behavioral therapies is the importance given to cognitive processes. Whereas behaviorists typically ignored beliefs, expectations, and other cognitive functions, the cognitive therapists believe that thoughts fundamentally influence emotions and behavior.

The cognitive therapies include cognitive restructuring techniques, coping skills therapies, and problem solving therapies.[8] Certain areas of shared beliefs unite these approaches. These beliefs suggest that adaptive and maladaptive behavioral patterns are mediated by cognition. In addition, they suggest that there are identifiable learning experiences that can activate or alter cognitive processes. Hence,

> [the] resultant task of the therapist is that of a diagnostician-educator who assesses maladaptive cognitive processes and subsequently arranges learning experiences

that will alter cognitions and the behavior and affect patterns with which they correlate. (p. 692)[8]

The *cognitive restructuring approaches*, also called systematic rational restructuring, are those approaches in which the therapist helps the client identify maladaptive thoughts, acknowledge their negative effects, and replace them with more adaptive patterns.[1,4,8,10] Rational-emotive therapy (RET)[3] is an example of these approaches. *Coping skills therapies* are a collection of diverse methods characterized by their focus on using techniques to help the individual deal (cope) with stressful situations.[5,8] They represent a new way of using existing techniques. A third category consists of *problem solving therapies*, which likewise contain varied principles and techniques. These focus on presenting a general way of approaching and dealing with a range of life problems.[2]

Cognitive approaches have been used effectively in the treatment of anxiety, anger, chronic pain, self-control, obesity, sexual dysfunction, and depression with a cognitive component.[6,9] They are believed to be helpful in treating obsessional thoughts, phobias, and, in general, (learned) neurotic disorders.[9] Cognitive approaches are not recommended for use with clients with limited ability to remember and express feelings and thoughts, those with difficulty recognizing the existence of personal problems, and those with limited ability to imagine solutions. The use of cognitive approaches is generally ruled out with individuals who are out of touch with reality and who cannot communicate. This may include most psychotic individuals, severely retarded people, drug abusers who are not reality oriented, very young children, and people who are severely brain damaged.[13] Specialized knowledge is required for use of cognitive therapy with children and adolescents.[6,10]

This chapter will highlight RET, one of the earliest cognitive therapies developed. It has been widely promoted through publications, workshops, and a training institute, and many clinicians are familiar with and use its methods. Therefore, RET stands as a popular example of the cognitive therapy approach.

HISTORY AND PURPOSE

Cognitive interventions arose from an attempt to find a synthesis between insight-oriented therapies and the behavioral movement. Whereas psychoanalytic and traditional psychotherapies focused on the development of insight and merely assumed that behavioral change would follow, behavioral therapies emphasized observable changes in behavior, while ignoring unobservable mental processes. The cognitive approaches, as a meeting ground between these two polarities, take for granted the involvement of cognitive phenomena in behavior, and at the same time seek to incorporate experimentally derived behavioral interventions and scientifically based assessment of effectiveness.[6]

The earliest reference to a cognitive influence on behavior is credited to the Greek Stoic philosopher Epictetus, who observed in the first century A.D. that "men are disturbed not by things, but by the view which they take of them" (quoted in Ellis,[3] p. 167). This is the understanding that Adler achieved in 1911 as he branched out from close association with Freud and came to view human conflicts as grounded in distorted thinking. Adler's ideas eventually influenced European and American thinking and theorizing. Although others sporadically referred to the role of thinking in the development of mental illness, no systematic scheme of the relationship between cognition and behavior was proposed until 1955. Then, Ellis formally presented his ideas on rational psychotherapy.[11] In the 1970s literature on cognitive therapy proliferated, presenting a challenge to the strict behavioral views that explained behavior in stimulus-response terms and to behavioral ideas of environmental determinism. The thesis of these writings was that stimulus-response explanations of human behavior were unable to account for complex human actions, and that cognitions, or thoughts, were the primary determinants of emotion and behavior.[13] In part, the challenge to environmental determinism was the result of developing methods of self-control. This new focus on self-control opened the way for consideration of internal or cognitive mediating processes and a view of humans in a more complex, reciprocal relationship with the environment—called reciprocal determinism.[8] Further, behavioral scientists themselves were becoming more interested in "private events," or thoughts. Interestingly, although thought processes were beginning to be the target of behavioral therapies, they were considered and explained in traditional stimulus-response terminology.[8]

Interest in cognitive therapies spread to other mental health workers, as well as to the lay person. Ellis[3] and Beck,[1] among others, were particularly influential in promoting the development of cognitive models. In a short time span, the blending of cognitive and behavioral theories had taken place, and new models emphasizing the mediative role of cognitions in the influence on emotions and behavior were developed.[8]

VIEW OF ORDER

From the perspective of RET, humans are seen as being neither good nor bad. Humans are objectively viewed as limited, and acceptance of human limitations is believed to be important to a rational life-style. At the same time, people are seen as capable of creating and guiding their own lives. Thus, humans are important simply because they exist and are in most instances able to direct their lives, guided by experience and personal values. While individuals are limited, they nevertheless have creative potential. In particular, this potential is important in the creation of emotional states, or in how one responds to positive and negative life events. Humans have, if they choose, control over their emotions and the option to decide to deal with life rationally.[11] Thus, RET philosophy views humans as responsible for their emotions and behavior, as having the potential to create personal meaning, and as behaving in ways influenced by thought processes rather than determined by unconscious forces.[3,11]

This view of humans offers no description of an ideal state of order, because people are viewed as limited and fallible while still capable of being basically well-functioning. The well-functioning (ordered) person is simply one who chooses to act in ways compatible with life satisfaction and positive social interaction and who has a few intimate relationships and involvement in personally satisfying activity.[12]

VIEW OF DISORDER

Typical of the RET view of disorder is the belief that clients have faults in their thinking patterns. Ellis called these faulty thinking patterns irrational. By this, he meant that individuals tended to think of simple desires or wishes for approval, success, and so on as needs, or essential conditions, rather than as the "simple preferences" that they are. Such irrational thinking leads to the conclusion that one *must* have certain things, and that life is awful if these hoped for events do not occur. Ellis coined the term "awfulizing" to describe this irrational process.[3,11]

Ellis developed the ABC theory of personality (later expanded to the ABCDE model) to explain the relationship among thoughts, feelings, and behavior. The components of this model are:

A—activating event (e.g., "I'll have to tell my wife I've lost the house keys");

B—belief system (beliefs may be rational or irrational; e.g., "A husband should be more responsible; I'm a failure and she will think I am an oaf");

C—emotional consequences (largely created by B; e.g., "Now I'm really feeling like a dummy and I'm anxious");

D—disputation or rational challenges to B, which may eliminate disturbing Cs (e.g., "Anyone can misplace keys. That certainly does not mean I'm a dummy"); and

E—new effects, "a more rational philosophy, a level of affect compatible with effective problem solving"(p. 21)[12] (e.g., "I'll tell her my keys are misplaced, we'll look around for them, and if necessary make a new set").

Ellis theorizes that A does not directly cause C. The beliefs, thoughts, or meanings we attribute to events determine the relationship between the activating event and the emotional response. This emphasis on the intervening influence of the belief system on emotions and behavior is central to the RET approach.[3,12]

Ellis suggests that there are a limited number of basic irrational beliefs that are responsible for an individual's emotional discomfort. These irrational beliefs are characterized as: untrue, commanding, leading to disturbed emotions, and not helpful in meeting goals. Some of these result from a category of thinking that Ellis calls the "Major Musts":

I must: (do well, get approval, etc.)
You must: (treat me well, love me, etc.)
The world must: (give me what I want quickly and easily, treat me fairly, etc.). (p. 74)[12]

A core irrational belief reflects the notion that people can be evaluated or rated in terms of their worth, goodness, and so on, and that people have certain obligations or needs. For example, the beliefs that if one is not loved then life is awful, or that one must always be treated fairly by others, are typical core irrational beliefs.[12] These core beliefs are then embellished and individualized to reflect the particular circumstances of a person's life. Disorder thus becomes the use of invalidated, irrational thinking to deal with the events of daily life. The emotional outcome of this pattern of thinking is emotional distress.

The theory of RET acknowledges genetic, environmental, and sociocultural impacts on the development of irrational thinking but puts these in perspective by saying that genetic and environmental influences do not maintain irrational thinking—people do this to themselves by "self-indoctrination."[3,12] It is the "here and now" faulty thinking that needs to and can be abandoned. No excuses based on personal history or environmental influences are acceptable. The focus is the present and the future.

ACTION IMPLICATIONS

Cognitive treatment in RET consists of logical, straightforward challenging of irrational beliefs. It is directed toward changing "faulty thinking" and is guided by the ABC model. Activating events, the belief system (especially core irrational beliefs), and emotional consequences are identified, and the therapeutic change centers on the client's recognizing illogical thinking and learning to dispute irrational beliefs. Thus, the ultimate goal of the RET process is to help the client learn to become his or her own therapist.[3,12]

Ellis speaks of the use of the ABC model and how the focus of RET differs from other traditional psychotherapies:

Most major psychotherapies also concentrate either on A, the Activating Events in the individual's life or on C, the emotional Consequences experienced subsequent to the occurrence of these events. But this is precisely what the individual wrongheadedly does himself: over-focuses on A and/or C and rarely deeply considers B, his Belief System, which is the vital factor in the creation of his symptoms. (p. 178)[3]

The treatment process begins with some type of evaluation. This is probably the least developed area of RET, because there are few evaluations available that identify basic irrational ideas.[3,12] Information is gathered through the use of psychological tests, history-taking, and general discussion of the model components.[13] The therapist assumes that clients can identify their problems; this is in contrast to psychoanalytic approaches in which people are believed to be incapable of truly knowing what their problems are.

The therapist's role is typically active-directive, persuasive, straightforward, and challenging. This role combines a perception of the client as an individual with "a ruthless, hardheaded campaign against [the client's] self-defeating *ideas, traits,* and *performances*" (p. 169).[3]

The components of the treatment process include: (1) direct education and persuasion to the RET belief in irrational thoughts as the cause of distress; (2) use of the client to self-monitor thoughts; (3) therapist modeling of rational thinking; (4) use of straightforward feedback, challenge, confrontation, and redirection of client thoughts and beliefs; and (5) use of homework assignments and practice sessions in which new rational self-statements and behaviors are performed.[8] A variety of methods such as discussion, behavioral techniques, reading assignments, and audiovisuals are employed to achieve profound cognitive changes. All treatment techniques are aimed at enabling the client to replace a self-defeating outlook with a more tolerant life philosophy.[3] Typical of the cognitive restructuring techniques, RET helps people learn to identify and attack their irrational, perfectionistic thoughts, abandon absolutist thinking, and be more realistic about human limitations.[3]

CRITICISMS AND LIMITATIONS

A major criticism of the cognitive body of knowledge is that research is inadequate to determine the relative effectiveness of cognitive and behavioral techniques for achieving change. Currently research support for behavioral techniques appears to outweigh that for cognitive techniques.[7]

Another criticism concerns the combining of cognitive and behavioral practice models. Debate continues over the degree to which these approaches can or should be combined to accurately reflect the complexity of human functioning.[8,14]

Finally, the population which can benefit from these techniques is clearly limited to a reality-oriented, insightful, and verbally expressive population.

COMMENTARY

Occupational therapists seek to understand persons' occupational performances in the context of their values, interests, and sense of effectiveness in daily life. These motivational components may reflect and interact with belief systems, whether faulty or rational. As such, occupational therapy and cognitive techniques can be complementary, supporting therapies. Occupational therapists already use some of the techniques developed by cognitive therapists. This is particularly true in the area of developing interpersonal skills. Thus, both occupational and cognitive therapists can work together to reinforce therapeutic goals related to enhancing the patient's sense of control in life, to learning more adaptive ways to interact socially, and to recognizing and acknowledging one's abilities, strengths, successes, and potentials. In the area of identifying personally valued ideas, as opposed to family or culturally promoted ideas, both cognitive and occupational therapists intervene to help the client to clarify and to enact personal values.

As the cognitive therapist helps the client to identify the thought processes that are impeding satisfying participation in life, the occupational therapist can challenge the client to explore and learn more about his or her abilities and everyday behavior. Both therapies share a common focus on the present and future and an emphasis on positive ways to be involved in and interpret the meaning of life events.

SUMMARY

History and Purpose	Cognitive approaches to therapy all share concern for the influence that cognitive functions have on affect and behavior. While their relationship to behaviorism is debatable, many acknowledge that cognitive therapies developed from discontent with behaviorists' general disregard of the effect that cognitive processes have on emotion and behavior. This examination of the role of thoughts on emotions and behavior emerged in the 1960s.

View of Order	In RET, individuals are viewed as limited by their humanity, yet possessing creative potential, enabling much individual control over emotional states and life choices. An ordered or well-functioning person chooses to act in ways compatible with: life satisfaction; positive social interaction; having a few intimate relationships; and involvement in personally satisfying activities.
View of Disorder	According to RET, the use of invalidated, irrational thinking to deal with the events of daily life constitutes disorder. The emotional outcome is distress.
Action Implications	The RET treatment process is directed toward changing faulty thought patterns and is guided by the ABC model of personality. The therapist directly challenges the client's maladaptive beliefs. Treatment aims at helping the client learn to be his own therapist.
Criticisms and Limitations	One criticism of cognitive approaches concerns the lack of evidence of clinical effectiveness to support a major role for cognitions in influencing behavior. Another major criticism concerns the relationship to behaviorism and the degree to which models of human functioning should reflect cognitive and behavioral events to accurately describe complex human functioning. Finally, cognitive therapies are limited, serving a reality-oriented, insightful, and verbally expressive population.
Commentary	Occupational therapists should have general knowledge of cognitive approaches as a complementary, supporting therapy. Occupational therapists already use some cognitive techniques. The two approaches can be used compatibly with clients to enhance their sense of control; to learn socially adaptive routines; and to confront values, abilities, strengths, successes, and potentials. Primarily, the cognitive therapist may help identify faulty thought processes while the occupational therapist can challenge clients to explore and learn about their abilities and their everyday behavior.

TERMS AND CONCEPTS

ABC theory the personality theory on which RET is based in which the relationship among thoughts, feelings, and behavior is explained. It has been expanded to the ABCDE model. The components of the model are: A-Activating events; B—Belief system; C—emotional Consequences; D—Disputation or rational challenges to B; and E—new Effects.

"awfulizing" a coined term used to describe irrational thought processes.

cognitions conscious thought processes such as beliefs, attributions, expectations, and assumptions.

cognitive restructuring a category of cognitive therapy in which the therapist helps the client identify maladaptive thoughts, acknowledge their negative effects, and replace them with more adaptive patterns. Also called systematic rational restructuring. Rational-emotive therapy is one example of this type of therapy.

cognitive therapies a collection of varied therapy techniques from divergent traditions all sharing concern for the impact that cognitive functions have on affect and behavior. In a pure sense, cognitive therapists believe that changes in cognitions will lead to changes in affect and behavior. These are also called semantic therapies and include: cognitive restructuring therapies, coping skills therapies, and problem solving therapies.

coping skills therapies a category of cognitive therapy containing a collection of diverse methods characterized by their focus on using techniques to help the individual deal (cope) with stressful life situations.

irrational thoughts a term used in RET for thought patterns that reflect personal beliefs that are unrealistic, illogical, or exaggerated in importance. Such thinking leads to emotional discomfort.

97

problem solving	a category of cognitive therapy containing varied
therapies	principles and techniques that focus on presenting
	a way to approach and deal with a range of life
	problems.

rational emotive	a cognitive restructuring therapy developed by Albert
therapy (RET)	Ellis in the 1950s in which people are considered
	responsible for their emotions and behavior, able to
	lead creative lives and behave in ways influenced
	by thought processes, not by unconscious forces.
	This approach is characterized by emphasis on the
	intervening influence of personal belief systems on
	emotions and behavior. Treatment consists of direct
	challenging of the interfering beliefs.

REFERENCES

1. Beck, A. T. *Cognitive therapy and the emotional disorders.* New York: International Universities Press, 1976.
2. D'Zurilla, T. J., & Goldfried, M. R. Problem solving and behavior modification. *Journal of Abnormal Psychology*, 1971, 78, 107–126.
3. Ellis, A. Rational-emotive therapy. In R. Corsini (Ed.), *Current psychotherapies.* Itasca, Ill.: F. E. Peacock, Publishers, 1973.
4. Goldfried, M. R., & Goldfried, A. P. Cognitive change methods. In F. H. Kanfer & A. P. Goldstein (Eds.), *Helping people change.* New York: Pergamon, 1975.
5. Kanfer, F. H. Self-management methods. In F. H. Kanfer & A. P. Goldstein (Eds.), *Helping people change.* New York: Pergamon Press, 1975.
6. Kendall, P. C., & Hollon, S. D. (Eds.). *Cognitive-behavioral interventions: Theory, research, and procedures.* New York: Academic Press, 1979.
7. Ledwidge, B. Cognitive behavior modification: A step in the wrong direction? *Psychological Bulletin*, 1978, 85, 353–375.
8. Mahoney, M. J., & Arnkoff, D. B. Cognitive and self-control therapies. In S. I. Garfield & A. E. Bergin (Eds.), *Handbook of psychotherapy and behavior change: An empirical analysis* (2nd ed.). New York: John Wiley and Sons, 1978.
9. McMullin, R. E., & Giles, T. R. *Cognitive-behavior therapy: A restructuring approach.* New York: Grune & Stratton, 1981.
10. Meichenbaum, P. Self-instructional methods. In F. H. Kanfer & A. P. Goldstein (Eds.), *Helping people change.* New York: Pergamon Press, 1975.

11. Morris, K. T., & Kanitz, H. M. *Rational-emotive therapy*. Boston: Houghton Mifflin, 1975.
12. Walen, S. R., DiGiuseppe, R., & Wessler, R. L. *A practitioner's guide to rational-emotive therapy*. New York: Oxford University Press, 1980.
13. Werner, H. D. *Cognitive therapy: A humanistic approach*. New York: The Free Press, 1982.
14. Wilson, T. G. Cognitive behavior therapy: Paradigm shift or passing phase? In J. B. Foreyt & D. P. Rathjen (Eds.), *Cognitive behavior therapy: Research and application*. New York: Plenum Press, 1978.

ADDITIONAL READINGS

Ellis, A. The basic clinical theory of RET. In A. Ellis & R. Grieger (Eds.), *Handbook of RET*. New York: Springer, 1977.

Lazarus, A., & Fay, A. *I can if I want to*. New York: Warner Books, 1977.

Mahoney, M. J. *Cognition and behavior modification*. Cambridge, Mass.: Ballinger Publishing Co., 1974.

Schwartz, A. *The behavior therapies: Theories and applications*. New York: The Free Press, 1982.

7
Reality Therapy

Reality therapy is an approach to behavior change developed by William Glasser in the 1950s. It stresses the responsibility that individuals should take for their own behavior. It also focuses on current behavior and on specific planning for more responsible future actions.[4,8] The therapeutic process depends on developing a relationship of caring involvement between the therapist and client, coupled with the therapist's consistent, firm requirement that clients clarify values and standards for behavior and judge their own behaviors as responsible or irresponsible.[8] Reality therapy deliberately deemphasizes psychiatric diagnostic labels. Psychosocial health and illness are understood primarily as manifestations of responsible or irresponsible behavior.[5] Reality therapy "depends upon what might be called a psychiatric version of the three R's, namely, *reality*, *responsibility*, and *right-and-wrong*" (p. xii).[9] Reality therapy is considered to be a commonsense therapy, easily learned and applicable to a wide range of people in a variety of situations.[8] Its principles have been used widely with delinquent and emotionally disturbed adolescents. They have been broadly applied to grade school classes as preventive intervention to promote successful identities in young children and to prevent failure and irresponsible behavior.[6] They have been successfully used in individual and group therapy for bereavement, marital discord, anxiety, and psychosis. Because it depends on a flow of effective communication, reality therapy is of little benefit to autistic or severely retarded clients.[8] The format for its use varies from group and individual psychotherapy to classroom discussion groups. Likewise, reality therapy principles are used in a wide range of settings, from mental hospitals to correctional facilities, halfway houses, and schools.[2]

HISTORY AND PURPOSE

Glasser considers reality therapy to be his unique creation which happens to be compatible with the thinking of several predecessors. For instance, the

Swiss physician Paul DuBois emphasized the role of the physician as an interested "friendly counselor," in which he helped the patient to focus on healthy thoughts as a replacement for ruminations on illness. Many similar early 20th century themes that emphasize healthy behavior and the sincere, friendly therapist presage modern reality therapy principles.[8] For instance, Adolf Meyer, an American psychiatrist, promoted such a commonsense approach, which stressed reality and responsibility. However, Glasser argues that the intervening "pansexual views" of Sigmund Freud came to overshadow these rational approaches.[8]

Reality therapy represents a reaction to many Freudian-oriented teachings. While in a psychiatric residency, Glasser and his supervisor, Harrington, who both shared doubts about traditional psychotherapy, jointly developed and applied the concepts of reality therapy with chronically psychotic veterans and seriously delinquent adolescent girls. Both programs were viewed as successful and led to applications in school settings and to the founding of the Institute for Reality Therapy. The reality therapy principles that grew out of this process are described in *Reality Therapy*[5] and *Schools Without Failure*.[6] The latest concern of reality therapy is with societal changes in the Western world around the 1950s. As the focus of contemporary life has moved from an emphasis on individual achievement (a job, diploma, etc.) to a concern with meaningful life roles, there have been corresponding repercussions in family life, the experience and meaning of success and failure, and those major institutions that deal with people experiencing chronic failures—the welfare system, hospitals, and the justice system. These changes have concomitantly affected the thinking and focuses of reality therapists.[7]

In comparing reality therapy with traditional analytically oriented psychotherapy, Glasser aims to invalidate the latter's claims of effectiveness. He states six points of reality therapy that are in fundamental disagreement with traditional psychotherapy:

1. Because we do not accept the concept of mental illness, the patient cannot become involved with us as a mentally ill person who has no responsiblity for his behavior.
2. Working in the present and toward the future, we do not get involved with the patient's history because we can neither change what happened to him nor accept the fact that he is limited by his past.
3. We relate to patients as ourselves, not as transference figures.
4. We do not look for unconscious conflicts or the reasons for them. A patient cannot become involved with us by excusing his behavior on the basis of unconscious motivations
5. We emphasize the morality of behavior. We face the issue of right and wrong which we believe solidifies the involvement, in contrast to conventional psy-

chiatrists who do not make the distinction between right and wrong, feeling it would be detrimental to attaining the transference relationship they seek.

6. We teach patients better ways to fulfill their needs. The proper involvement will not be maintained unless the patient is helped to find more satisfactory patterns of behavior. Conventional therapists do not feel that teaching better behavior is a part of therapy. (p. 54)[5]

It is evident from these statements that reality therapy is radically different from conventional therapy.

Reality therapy is, in a sense, a very conservative approach, taking a stand on what is right and wrong and doggedly returning responsibility to the client. This is in contrast to many new therapies which stress the relativity of morality.

Although the principles have been developed by psychiatrists, current practitioners of reality therapy include such professionals as psychologists, clergymen, social workers, teachers, probation officers, nurses, policemen, lawyers, and judges.[8]

VIEW OF ORDER

Early in his career and before he formulated the principles of reality therapy, Glasser stated this basic assumption: "We are often given the illusion that we can change our surroundings when in fact either they change in their own inconsistent pattern and/or we change our position relative to the world" (p. 8).[4] Glasser's view of order stresses individual responsibility, the ability to take control of one's life and to change one's own behavior, and the inability to change other people to make them fulfill one's personal needs. The only alternatives to facing reality and acting responsibly are to change our surroundings by moving to another location (e.g., changing jobs) or to try to make others change to meet our needs. However, because personal needs still exist regardless of where we live or work and because we have little real power to change other people, Glasser concludes that people must face reality and accept control of their own lives, learn to meet their own needs appropriately, and act responsibly on their knowledge of reality.

The concept of identity is the first and most basic idea of reality therapy. It reflects the universal need of all people to feel unique. People have either a success identity or a failure identity, based on feedback from social interactions and personal experiences with people and objects. This self-image may or may not be the same view that others have of us; it is highly personal. Glasser and Zunin[8] assert that this identity forms at the age of 4 to 5 years. They note that people with success identities associate with others with success identities, and, similarly, those with failure identities seek the company of like peers. Thus, success breeds success, and failure breeds failure.

Individuals with success identities are believed to possess two traits. First, they know that at least one other person in the world loves them, and they love that person in return. Second, they know that they are worthwhile individuals and that at least one other person believes this to be true also. Those with failure identities share the common experience of loneliness and deal with this discomfort by either denying reality or ignoring it.[8] Therefore, the concept of order in reality therapy is directly related to an individual's self-image, or success identity, which is revealed in the way a person behaves—responsibly or irresponsibly.

The second major concept is responsibility, a pervasive theme in reality therapy. It is defined as "the ability to fulfill one's needs, and to do so in a way that does not deprive others of the ability to fulfill their needs" (p. 15).[5] Behaving responsibly enhances feelings of self-worth and one's sense of value to others. Responsibility is learned through a caring, involved relationship, and as one demonstrates the ability to handle limited responsibility, one is challenged to accept more responsibility and achieve new successes.[5]

Involvement is a third important concept. It is the process by which people naturally fulfill needs and develop self-images as successes. Involvement also refers to the genuine, caring therapist/client relationship (*not* as a transference relationship) and is also importantly recognized as the process through which therapeutic gains will be maintained after termination of treatment. Glasser and Zunin see the need for involvement as "the primary intrinsic driving force governing all behavior" (p. 296).[8]

These principles suggest a view of humans as self-determined; that is, given an individual's assets and limitations of biological and psychological inheritance and of the environment, people can make of themselves what they will. People are what they do, and they have a vast capacity to behave in many different ways. The way in which one behaves "depends upon decisions rather than conditions" (p. 306).[8] Glasser and Zunin further state that each person has a "health or growth force," meaning that people naturally want and strive toward successes, responsible behavior, and meaningful relationships with others (p. 297).[8]

VIEW OF DISORDER

Glasser disagrees with the concept of "mental illness" and prefers the medical analogy of "weakness" rather than "illness." Ideally, he would like to totally dispense with diagnosis and refer to all clients as simply irresponsible. In Glasser's view, all psychosocial disorders emanate from irresponsible behavior, leading to a lack of need fulfillment and unhappiness.[4,5] Irresponsible people either deny or ignore reality and consequently are unable to meet their own needs. The resulting behavior has been popularly called mental illness. People with a psychosis deny reality by viewing the world through their own private fantasy for the purpose of self-protection from feeling lonely and worthless. Those called delinquent, sociopathic, and personality disordered are all basically antisocial in their disregard of society's rules. They simply ignore the reality that they know exists.[8] Glasser and Zunin summarize the view of etiology in the assertion that "unhappiness is the result and not the cause of irresponsibility" (p. 292).[8]

This unconventional view of etiology suggests that people develop emotional discomfort "because their performance has been, and is, too low" (pp. xiii–xiv)[9] rather than because their standards have been excessively high; thus, the goal of therapy is to increase one's accomplishments. This *under*socialization is the basic problem in disorder, and it is manifested in irresponsibility and the failure to make commitments and the accompanying sacrifices required to achieve goals.[9]

ACTION IMPLICATIONS

Reality therapy attempts to challenge the client to be responsible, to make commitments, and, consequently, to achieve more. Its concepts are all designed to accomplish these goals, with the anticipated result that people who once viewed themselves as failures will accept increasing responsibility, accumulate accomplishments, and begin to feel successful. Persons with all diagnoses are treated using basically the same process to help the person to "fulfill his needs in the real world so that he will have no inclination in the future to deny its existence" (p. 7).[5] In short, the therapist teaches responsibility to those who did not learn it early in life.

Reality therapy is best described as a philosophy of treatment and a process of therapy rather than as a collection of techniques. A variety of accepted techniques such as role playing, contracting, and homework assignments may be used, but only as they fit within the basic philosophy of individual responsibility for behavior and the caring and involved relationship with the client.

Glasser and Zunin describe the reality therapy process as based on eight principles. First, the therapist is involved and cares; thus therapy is personal. Involvement takes place as the therapist relates to the client as a caring, genuine, and real person who acts to demonstrate responsibility and insists on the client's acting responsibly, while maintaining the caring relationship—a subtle and delicate balance.[5] The therapist is willing to share personal experiences and is open to having his or her values and standards challenged.

Second, the focus of therapy is on behavior and not feelings, because it has been observed that it is easier to intervene in a cycle of negative events through *doing* something different rather than by first *feeling* something different. Behavior is believed to be easier for an individual to control than feelings. Third, therapy deals mainly with the present. The past cannot be changed, and too much time is typically spent dwelling on past failures. In dealing with the present and future, discussion can turn to the more positive direction of what people are doing or can do to improve their situations. Fourth, reality therapists deal with value judgments. They expect clients to identify goals, values, and standards for behavior and to measure their own behavior against these. A fifth principle is that of planning. Once the client identifies general directions and ways to change behavior, the therapist has the client specify this change in terms of when, where, and with whom. The sixth principle is commitment. Early in therapy, the therapist encourages the client to follow through with plans "for the therapist" and later "for him- or herself." In both cases a commitment to action is required. The seventh principle simply states that no excuses are acceptable. The therapist realizes that plans fail at times, but concern is only for when the plan or an alternative will be tried again, not for the reasons of failure. The eighth and final principle is that of eliminating punishment. Punishment is not an effective way to help people with poor self-images to change.[5,8]

In addition to these eight principles, there are five identified stages of therapy that guide the client to clarify values, goals, and standards for behavior; to identify behaviors that interfere with their accomplishment; and to generate alternate behaviors.[1,8]

First, the problem solving process is initiated by asking "What are you doing?" and probing for details such as "What happened? Where? When? How?" but not "Why?" In the second stage, the therapist asks if the client's past actions accomplished any good. This question is commonly met with resistance. Thus, the therapist must be involved with the client if the client is to respond honestly to this crucial question. If the client maintains that he or she acted properly and would continue to behave in the same way, the therapist leaves the issue until the client expresses a desire to alter the behavior. Self-evaluation of behavior is essential since individual responsibility is the core of therapy. If the client admits that a behavior is negative, therapy continues, focusing on that behavior.

Assuming therapy progresses, the third stage begins the process of relearning as the therapist asks what the client's plan is for changing behavior. The plan of action is "pinned down." Alternatives are considered through a brainstorming process, role playing may be used, and future strategies, times, places, and backup plans are specified in detail. In the fourth and fifth stages, a contract stating details of the plan for behavior such as time, place, and so on is signed by the client and a follow-up session is scheduled for the client to report how the plan went or to revise the plan if necessary.[1]

Therapy may involve a lively verbal exchange, with the emphasis always on the client's positive points and potentials. The therapist's role is more like a teacher than a traditional therapist, and as such, the therapist is willing to be a real person, revealing personal information and being open to having values and opinions challenged.[1,5,8] Humor, confrontation, and debates may occur. Conversational content will likely range over a wide array of daily events as the therapist and client identify problems of social interaction and seek alternate ways for the client to become meaningfully involved with others.[8] As Glasser states, "When values, standards, and responsibility are in the background, all discussion is relevant to therapy. Continually stressing responsibility is artificial" (p. 38).[5]

The pivotal issue on which behavior change hinges is identifying the client's values:

> Where standards and values are not stressed, the most that therapy can accomplish is to help patients become more comfortable in their irresponsibility. Because our effort is always directed toward helping patients fulfill their needs, we insist on their striving to reach the highest possible standards. (p. 72)[5]

Thus, reality therapy involves a strong element of challenge to help the client live up to self-professed standards. The client maintains control of the pace of therapy by deciding whether or not to acknowledge irresponsible behavior. The therapist remains available to help at any time the client wishes to work further. Ideally, the trust nurtured through involvement, coupled with the client's natural urge to grow, will lead to change.

CRITICISMS AND LIMITATIONS

The point of view taken in reality therapy is typically in opposition to stands taken by two groups: (1) traditional psychoanalytically oriented individuals and (2) those who claim that there is an overemphasis on individual responsibility for personal misfortune when environmental factors may be more to blame. Those from a more classic psychoanalytic position are opposed to Glasser's stand that mental illness does not exist and criticize him for denying the emotional suffering of psychosocially dysfunctional persons. His unconventional theory and rebellion against traditional concepts of psychotherapy have resulted in a lack of support from some in the academic community who do not agree with his basic views of human behavior and its determinants.[10]

There has also been criticism of approaches to health care which emphasize the responsibility of the individual with a psychosocial problem who may be the "victim" of such factors as poverty, poor parenting, and the like. "Blaming the victim" is the phrase used to refer to these approaches. While the critics have not singled out Glasser's work per se, their criticisms appear to be relevant. In stressing the responsibility of the patient (especially with younger, poorer, and otherwise relatively powerless clients), the therapist may be overlooking familial and environmental factors that made the person's maladaptive behavior understandable and contributed to its maintenance. To the degree that the person is enjoined to shoulder all the responsibility, the responsibility that belongs to family, social agencies, and the like is ignored.[3,11]

A limitation of reality therapy is that it is not a complete system of treatment. Rather, it is a well-developed philosophy, with few clearly associated treatment techniques. Thus, practitioners are left to draw on a wide array of other techniques and apply them within their understanding of the theory. Glasser also notes the limitation of his theories to the Western culture and value system in which they were developed. In relationship to evaluations of treatment effectiveness, Glasser and Zunin note that research sophistication has not developed to a degree of refinement to meaningfully measure variables influenced by reality therapy.[8] While recidivism declined at the school for delinquent girls where reality therapy was applied, no controlled, long-term research study of outpatients has been conducted.[8] Overall, little research exists to support claims of treatment effectiveness.

Because reality therapy is primarily a verbal therapy, its application is limited to verbal, cognitively able clients. Another implication of the primarily verbal nature of reality therapy is that it involves talking about doing (i.e., planning for doing) but does not focus on learning skills for action.

COMMENTARY

Many of the themes of reality therapy are highly compatible with occupational therapy. The focus on establishing a relationship with the client where the therapist is a real multifaceted person (i.e., not a transference figure) is shared by both occupational therapy and reality therapy. Similarly, concern with providing a supportive, nonthreatening, but challenging environment for growth and the companion emphasis on the positive aspects of the client are common to both. Neither occupational therapy nor reality therapy encourages acting out negative behaviors. Instead, both encourage the development and expression of positive reality-based, socially acceptable, and need-satisfying actions. Both therapies approach clients with a challenging spirit to help them live up to their standards, fulfill their potential, and respond positively with accomplishment to the urge to grow and become competent. The reality therapy manner of introducing challenge to the patient and the dogged insistence that the patient plan and make a commitment to action are of special interest, since this theme of challenge is a shared philosophical area of agreement between the therapies. In occupational therapy practice, therapists might find the reality therapy orientation to be a useful guide for operationalizing the ideals of challenge and demands for performance in the clinic.

The focus on doing over feelings, behavior over attitudes, and the present and future over the past are common to both occupational therapy and reality therapy. Because of the compatibility of these themes, the shared common-sense orientation, and common interest in everyday situations as the content of therapy, the therapies may sound similar. However, there is one important difference. Reality therapy is a verbal therapy with homework assignments. Occupational therapy is activity-oriented and typically provides a setting for "hands-on" involvement in activities in which clients can test their abilities and become aware of the impact of these experiences on self-image. Therefore, there is potential for reality therapy and occupational therapy to be effectively used together.

SUMMARY

History and Purpose	Reality therapy is a commonsense approach to behavior change emphasizing reality and responsibility. It was developed by William Glasser in the 1950s in reaction to many Freudian-oriented teachings. It stresses the responsibility that individuals should take for their own behavior, current behavior, and specific planning for future actions.
View of Order	Humans naturally desire successful self-images and responsibility through a caring involvement with others. The formation of a successful self-image depends on being actively involved with others, meeting individual needs, and making responsible choices and actions.
View of Disorder	Individual diagnoses are not considered useful labels. All people with psychosocial disorders are viewed as irresponsible in their acknowledgement of reality. This irresponsibility leads to unhappiness as people either deny or ignore reality and are, thus, unable to meet their needs.

Action Implications	Reality therapy philosophy promotes individual responsibility for behavior and asserts the value of involvement with others to learn and maintain responsible behavior. A variety of techniques such as role playing, contracting, and homework assignments may be used, but only as they fit with the basic philosophy. Reality therapy attempts to challenge the client to be responsible, acknowledge personal values, make commitments, and achieve more. The key event on which behavior change is dependent is the acknowledgement of personal values.
Criticisms and Limitations	Reality therapy is criticized for denying the existence of painful emotional disturbance and overemphasizing individual responsibility when environmental factors may be more to blame. Its limitations include a lack of clearly associated treatment techniques, a lack of research, and the sole use of verbal therapy.
Commentary	Occupational therapy and reality therapy are compatible treatment approaches. Areas of agreement include establishing a genuine, caring client/therapist relationship; providing a supportive yet challenging environment for growth; focusing on health and positive issues; encouraging reality-based need-satisfying actions; and emphasizing doing in the present. The critical difference is in the treatment applications. Reality therapists work through verbal means. Occupational therapists use activities.

TERMS AND CONCEPTS

"blaming the victim" a phrase used by critics of treatment approaches that stress individual responsibility to refer to the unwarranted burdening of individuals (or clients) with responsibility for life events that have been beyond the individual's control.

failure identity an individual's self-image based on feelings of loneliness. Individuals with failure identities tend to deny or ignore reality as a way to cope with loneliness. Glasser believes that this self-image is formed by 4–5 years of age.

identity the basic cross-cultural need of all people to feel unique.

involvement the process by which people naturally fulfill needs and develop self-images as successes or failures. It refers to the genuine relationship with another person. The need for involvement is believed by reality therapists to be the intrinsic force behind all behavior.

irresponsible behavior the choices and actions that do not lead to need fulfillment or are disruptive to others' need fulfillment and lead to unhappiness, as people either deny or ignore reality and are unable to meet personal needs. Irresponsible behaviors are deemed the source of all psychosocial disorders.

responsibility the ability to meet individual needs while not interfering with others' ability to fulfill needs.

success identity an individual's self-image based on the knowledge that one is loved and that one loves others in return and that one feels worthwhile. Glasser believes that it is formed by 4–5 years of age.

REFERENCES

1. Bassin, A. The reality therapy paradigm. In A. Bassin, T. E. Bratter, & R. L. Rachin (Eds.), *The reality therapy reader: A survey of the work of William Glasser, M.D.* New York: Harper & Row, 1976.
2. Bassin, A., Bratter, T. E., & Rachin, R. L. (Eds.). *The reality therapy*

reader: A survey of the work of William Glasser, M.D. New York: Harper & Row, 1976.

3. Gaylin, W., Glasser, I., Marchus, S., & Rothman, D. *Doing good: The limits of benevolence.* New York: Pantheon Books, 1978.

4. Glasser, W. *Mental health or mental illness? Psychiatry for practical action.* New York: Harper & Row, 1960.

5. Glasser, W. *Reality therapy: A new approach to psychiatry.* New York: Perennial Library/Harper & Row, 1975.

6. Glasser, W. *Schools without failure.* New York: Harper & Row, 1969.

7. Glasser, W. *The identity society* (rev. ed.). New York: Harper & Row, 1972/75.

8. Glasser, W., & Zunin, L. M. Reality therapy. In R. Corsini (Ed.), *Current psychotherapies.* Itasca, Ill.: F. E. Peacock Publishers, 1973.

9. Mowrer, O. H. Foreword, in Glasser, W. *Reality therapy: A new approach to psychiatry.* New York: Perennial Library/Harper & Row, 1975.

10. Reilly, S. Dr. Glasser without failure. In A. Bassin, T. E. Bratter, & R. L. Rachin (Eds.), *The reality therapy reader: A survey of the work of William Glasser, M.D.* New York: Harper & Row, 1976.

11. Ryan, W. *Blaming the victim.* New York: Pantheon Books, 1971.

8

Communications/Interaction Theory

Communications/interaction theory is a relatively new body of knowledge that has arisen largely out of an attempt to understand the peculiar speech and thought patterns of people with schizophrenia. The stance of this theory is that behavior can be fully understood only if it is examined as part of the larger context, or framework, in which it is contained. This position is summarized by the following:

> A phenomenon remains unexplainable as long as the range of observation is not wide enough to include the context in which the phenomenon occurs. (p. 21)[13]

Because the context for most behavior generally involves relationships between and among people, this tradition of knowledge has been primarily concerned with seeking interpersonal or interactional explanations of disorder. Hence, its initial target client population was families with schizophrenic members, rather than schizophrenic persons themselves. However, many of the principles of treatment associated with this school have been more recently used with individual clients representing a variety of disorders.

HISTORY AND PURPOSE

Classical psychoanalysis (see Chapter 2) sought to explain behavior as individuals' attempts to satisfy inner needs or drives. Eventually, dissatisfaction with this exclusively inner-determined view of behavior led neo-Freudian theorists (see Chapter 3) to propose more socially or culturally oriented ex-

---

In some ways a confusing body of knowledge, the concepts in this tradition have frequently included new terminology, or used old, familiar terms in new and unusual ways. Whenever possible, this chapter will avoid this semantic problem by using more mundane ways of expressing the same ideas.

planations of behavior. Simultaneously, behaviorists were proceeding from the opposite direction, suggesting that behavior was a response to environmental stimuli (see Chapter 5). In all of these accounts, however, more emphasis was placed on explaining isolated acts of isolated individuals than on explaining patterns of behavior occurring during interactions between people. Further, these theories relied on relatively simple cause-and-effect explanations of behavior. For example, prolonged separation from one's mother during infancy was seen as the cause of becoming an insecure and untrusting adult. In addition, Freudian and neo-Freudian theories endowed people with inner structures, such as the superego or the id, that took on a life of their own.[13]

In the mid-twentieth century, the increased application of systems theory to the natural sciences and the development of information theory influenced an interdisciplinary group of social and behavioral scientists to begin describing both ordered and disordered human behavior purely in terms of patterns of interpersonal relationships. Because communication comprises the concrete or "observable manifestations of relationships" (p. 21),[13] a critical focus of this group was verbal and nonverbal communication. Along with the focus on observable events, communications/interaction theorists sought to understand the "what" and "how" of an event, instead of the "why," thereby precluding concern with mysterious inner structures as explanations of motivation and behavior.

VIEW OF ORDER

The view of order in this body of knowledge draws on four theoretical sources: information theory, cybernetics, systems theory, and Russel's Theory of Logical Types. Communications/interaction theorists have integrated ideas and concepts from these theories to develop an orientation to human behavior summarized by the belief that behavior can only be understood in the context of relationships.

Behavior as Information

Information theory enables human behavior to be seen as a process of "information exchange." What this means is that behavior is viewed as information passing between individuals as they act and react with reference to each other.[13] To amplify the notion of behavior as information, communications/interaction theories turned to the cybernetic concept of feedback.

Cybernetic theory focuses on processes of feedback and how they modify behavior. A common cybernetic process is the thermostat, which reads the temperature of the room (feedback) and, based on its reading, turns on or off a furnace or air conditioner (behavior) to achieve a preset goal. Such cybernetic processes of aiming for a goal, using feedback to monitor progress toward or maintenance of the goal, and altering ongoing behavior based on feedback are identified as an integral part of the information exchange that takes place when people interact. Thus, interaction and communication are circular processes in which one person transmits some "information" to another person, who then receives and reacts to this information. This reaction in turn sends new information to the first person. Each of the parties in the relationship continually judges the received information to determine whether or not it fits into his or her schema of acceptable responses.[13]

Because communication is a circular process, it is not always clear who is the initiator and who the respondent in a sequence of events. However, because people tend to look for beginnings and endings in their interactions, they figuratively add periods to the sequence of events in which they engage.[13] These figurative periods establish one event as beginning an interaction and another as a response to the first event. Thus, in some relationships, one person will consider his or her actions to always be a response to another's. For example, at the doctor's office, the patient frequently considers the doctor to be leading or directing the interaction. Similarly, one country may consider its escalation policies to be in response to another country's initiation of an arms build-up. In other situations, perhaps a problem-solving group, all parties may feel that they are equally leading and following.

Information exchange and feedback processes are used to explain how behavior and the external social order become stable, and thus accepted and expected by persons. The events of human behavior are recurrent; that is, they occur on a fairly routine basis in a fairly predictable fashion, giving out a constant stream of information about what behavior is acceptable in our social and cultural world. These repeated and recognizable patterns are construed by most people as indicative of normal or ordered behavior. For example, a pattern of ordered behavior in a relationship between an employer and employee may require the recognition that in this situation one person leads and another follows. Ordered behavior in other situations, however, may be characterized by equal leading and following on the part of both members of the relationship.[13]

Open Systems and Behavior

Systems theory adds a dynamic perspective to understanding behavior. Open systems theory seeks to go beyond the linear cause-and-effect thinking that characterizes closed systems concepts. An open system differs from a closed system in that it interacts with the environment and is capable of both maintaining and changing itself. As such, it is more complex than and incorporates cybernetic processes. Instead of maintaining a status quo, an open

115

system evolves as it takes in information from the environment and puts out certain behaviors. Every event that affects an open system changes it in some way; thus, a system's response to present events reflects its past experiences.

In the communications/interaction body of knowledge, the family is described as an open system that incorporates cybernetic processes and information exchange. Looking at the family as a system implies that the family is more than just a collection of individuals. It is, in fact, an organization that is characterized by certain recurring patterns of behavior and that influences and responds as a whole to the external environment.[5]

Because the family is an open system, events proceed in a circular, rather than a linear, fashion. This means that the same behavior or result may arise from different causes. For instance, a teen-aged boy may be late to dinner because he was still doing homework, watching television, or angry with his parents. Similarly, behavior is also multidetermined; that is, there is not simply one antecedent to one response. Thus, a previous fight with his father may have caused the son to be unable to concentrate on his homework and not finish before dinnertime. Finally, positive events occurring outside the family system (such as a good teacher in school) may modulate or alleviate effects of family processes, while stress (say, failing a test) may exacerbate them, causing a "snowball" effect.[5]

Within the family system, just as within society, particular patterns of interaction occur on a regular basis. These characteristic patterns prescribe internally acceptable ways for family members to interact with one another.[5] For instance, an accepted pattern of behavior in one family may be for the mother to make all decisions about how late children should stay up. According to communications/interaction theorists, such patterns are unique to each family and are not to be judged in terms of external standards or norms, but rather in terms of their productiveness for the particular family.

Logical Types

The fourth major source of ideas for communications/interaction theory is the concept of logical types. This concept is concerned with the meaning of the information that is shared by persons and the way in which meaning is changed or influenced by context. The concept of logical types refers to the idea that not all communication is of the same kind. For instance, the comment, "This was an interesting conversation," is a statement *about* the talk and is clearly different from the communication given *during* the talk itself. Context refers to the overall setting or scene of behavior.[1] As the scene changes, the same words may take on totally different meanings. Thus the phrase "I love you" has a vastly different meaning when said between two persons celebrating their thirtieth wedding anniversary, between a parent and child, or between two people on their second date. Similarly, the game of baseball takes on two completely different meanings when played by major league teams or played at a picnic.

According to the theory of logical types, the context represents a different level of communication from the message occurring within it. It is a higher, or more abstract, class of communication. This is the same notion we use when we categorize animals, for instance. Mammals are a class that contains cats and dogs among others. Once we recognize that a cat is a mammal we immediately know certain facts about cats that are shared by all mammals. In the same way, by knowing the context of a behavior, certain information is communicated to us which helps to explain that behavior. This level of communication, being on a higher level than the immediate behavior itself, is called metacommunication; it is communication *about* communication.[1]

People recognize and manipulate contexts every day. For example, when two children agree to "play house," they are in effect saying that they will communicate and behave within the context of playing house. Should one child say something or behave in a fashion that does not suit playing house or the respective roles of mother, father, or child, his or her playmate will recognize and object to this behavior. This use of contexts is carried into adult life when persons behave and communicate in such varied contexts as a classroom, party, theater, walking down a street, dining out, praying in temple, and so on.

Context is not the only form of metacommunication that exists. Nonverbal communication, such as gestures, facial expressions, and distances between people, is a form of metacommunication that helps to define the relationship between communicating individuals.[4,8,9,13] For instance, we accept that doctors can freely touch patients, but it is quite unlikely that a patient will initiate contact with a doctor (unless it is to prevent some dreaded event such as a shot). At work, subordinates are much less likely to touch their bosses than vice versa.[4]

Nonverbal communication may be consistent with or contradictory to the verbal message. At times, the relationship between the two may be deliberately contradictory; this is often the case in play, fantasy, ritual, and humor.[1] For example, if one child says to another, "Let's shake hands," and then laughingly pulls his or her hand away at the last minute, a joking context of contradictory messages has been created. Further, the nonverbal communication within one context may be deliberately contradictory to that within another. To use our example of children playing house, if one child says to another, "Let's play house—I'll be the mommy and you be the baby," although the message *within* the game is that the children are *not* equal, the reality of the play situation is that the children *are indeed partners.*

117

Order

Ordered behavior, as conceptualized by this school, involves several components. First, it is behavior that meets certain acceptable standards for a given situation. To do this, individuals must recognize what is appropriate and required in different contexts. Second, order involves the ability to shift contexts, both as demanded by changes in the environment, and to fulfill one's own interpersonal goals. Order also derives from the ability to recognize and shift between relationships that involve leading and following, or sharing these functions on an equal basis. Finally, order involves the recognition of both stated and unstated meanings of communication and the ability to deliberately use nonverbal communication to lend meaning to contexts.

Communications/interaction theory thus explains order in human behavior as a form of information exchange in which people send and receive messages from each other, mutually adjusting their behavior as they go along. This process is aided by the ability to recognize different levels of communication, or metacommunication. In particular, the context in which the communication occurs influences participants' behavior, at the same time that their behavior helps to maintain the context. Further, this context gives meaning to behaviors that might otherwise appear to be senseless or puzzling. Order therefore involves a number of complex factors that simultaneously and dynamically affect any human interaction. To illustrate how these processes are manifested in a simple interaction, consider the following episode:

> A man approaches a cashier in a store to purchase an item. He hands her the item while smiling and looking directly into her eyes. She takes the item, ringing up the price and announcing the total. He takes a check out of his wallet while asking whether he has met her before. She responds negatively, displaying her ringless finger. She asks for his address and phone number to put on the back of the check he wrote, and he asks if he might not also have hers.

In this sequence of events two episodes occur simultaneously: the purchase and the meeting of a potential date. Both give messages that imply and derive their meaning from the two contexts that surround the events. The first context, the store, is immediately apparent and requires the behaviors of buying an item and waiting at the cash register. The second context is made obvious by virtue of actions that are clearly outside and even unnecessary to the first context—the eye contact, showing a ringless hand, the question of whether they have met before (which is not taken as a literal question, but as an indication of his interest in her), and the final request for her phone number. While neither the cashier nor the customer may believe they have initiated the interaction, both may interpret the other's actions as feedback to continue. Finally, behavior which might be puzzling in the wrong context is expected and consistent once both individuals have acknowledged the existence of a second context (flirting).

VIEW OF DISORDER

Communications/interaction theorists were initially concerned with understanding schizophrenia as a symptom of disordered family communication. Although they have since generalized from this work to explain other forms of psychopathology, schizophrenia, as a communication problem, is the focal point of their discussion of disorder.

In a basic form, disordered communication involves disagreement or confusion between the verbal intent of a message and the metacommunication accompanying the same message.[13] When such contradictions exist, the other party to the communication does not know what response to make. Because the nonverbal part of the message essentially serves to define the relationship between the two parties, it can say to the other person, "I accept you and our relationship as you see it"; "I do not accept you or our relationship"; or "I neither accept nor unaccept you—this relationship does not exist." The first two messages, while not equally desirable, are clearly understood, but the third is confusing and mystifying.[13] It is this third category that characterizes disordered communication. For instance, if a student requests an appointment with a professor, and the professor says either "I will meet with you next Tuesday" or "I will not meet with you next Tuesday," the message to the student is unambiguous. However, if the professor says, "Just drop in during office hours," but has no defined office hours and is never there, the student has received two contradictory messages—one of the professor's availability and one of his or her inaccessibility.

Although most people encounter this type of situation on an occasional basis, in some families it persists as the norm. When such contradictory or *double-bind* messages typify family communication, a potential setting for the development of schizophrenia exists. Communications/interaction theorists believe that the double-bind situation epitomizes pathological family communication.

The double-bind has five necessary ingredients. First, it involves two or more persons, one of whom is thought of as the "victim." Second, the double-bind generally begins with a primary negative injunction or command. For example, the child is told, "If you do not do what I say, you will be punished." Next, another negative message is given which conflicts with the first. Thus, the second message is of the sort that says, "Even though I am punishing you, I really love you." This conflicting message may be conveyed by nonverbal means, or it may be created by disagreement between two controlling parties (for instance, when parents disagree about what behavior is expected of the child). The fourth ingredient pertains to the inability of the victim, or child, to leave the setting. The last ingredient of the double-bind is that the combination of events represents a recurrent pattern of interaction. As the double-bind structure becomes the norm and is habitually expected by the child, any part of the sequence will suffice to precipitate the feelings and reactions associated with the entire sequence.[1,3,5,11]

The typical example given of a double-bind is a situation in which a mother feels threatened and anxious when her child responds to her as a loving parent. Because such feelings of anxiety are unacceptable to her, she counteracts her discomfort or hostility by simulating loving behavior. The first negative message given the child is, "If you are too affectionate, I will withdraw" (punish you). The second message, directly contradicting the first is, "Mothers are supposed to be loving and affectionate, so I will pretend to be that way with you and you must pretend to believe me." Both these messages are more likely to be communicated through actions or nonverbal behavior than through words. Finally, the child has no choice in the situation, other than to accept the double-bind. Either she or he perceives the initial truth, which will certainly not be pleasant, or the child deceives him- or herself in order to avoid the unpleasant truth. But deceiving oneself means denying one's own internal perceptions. In other words, if the child accurately perceives that the mother does not want the child to be affectionate, she or he will be hurt. But denying this first message will cause him or her to be hurt anyway, when the mother does withdraw.[1]

Because people caught in a double-bind learn to deny their perceptions, they eventually do *not* learn to interpret or manipulate the metacommunicative levels of interaction in the same way that others do. Instead, these people develop various maneuvers or strategies for dealing with the double-bind. These strategies make sense in their own universe, but not in anyone else's. For instance, they may respond literally to a metaphoric message, such as tasting a nonfood substance upon being told that it looks good enough to eat. They may insist that they are not there or that they are somebody else. They may continually search for hidden meanings in what others say, or they may treat all messages as unimportant and laughable. Sometimes, schizophrenics may use language as an attempt to *not* communicate. Because both agreeing and disagreeing with the messages being sent is dangerous, they may try to do neither, by using vague, incoherent, or tangential speech. Ultimately, they may simply avoid responding to all messages. These strategies parallel the bizarre behaviors of the different schizophrenias—paranoia, hebephrenia, catatonia, and speech peculiarities.

Disorder in the person therefore emanates from disorder in the family, in particular, from the "no win" and "no way out" communication of the double-bind. The victim of the double-bind escapes only by denying the reality of the communication in some fashion and is thereby forced out of the world of reality as others experience it.

ACTION IMPLICATIONS

The goal of communications/interaction therapy is to enable the family to identify the patterns maintaining the double-bind situation(s). Family members can then find more effective solutions to their problems and can replace the disordered communication patterns.

The communications/interaction theorists differentiate between two types of change—first-order change and second-order change.[14] First-order change refers to change made *within* a given context and tends to involve "more-of-the-same" or "less-of-the-same" behaviors. For example, two children playing house might get into a fight over the proper role of the "mother." To solve the fight, they eventually agree that the "mother" should do some, but not all, of the disputed behaviors. Another example would be a student's decision to study longer hours for an exam because of a previously low grade. Second-order change, however, involves a change of context, and thus a reconceptualization of the entire situation. The two children playing house might therefore decide that another game would be more enjoyable. Similarly, the student who made a low grade might decide that the problem was not one of poor study habits, but one of nervousness, and that practicing yoga before the next test would be more useful than extra cramming. To some extent, second-order change appears illogical because the connection between the solution and the problem is not immediately apparent.

Second-order change often involves the therapist's use of paradoxical instructions. Paradoxical instructions include such methods as telling someone to advertise something she or he has been concealing, to do something she or he has been afraid will happen; prescribing the symptom itself; or perhaps giving conflicting sets of instructions to the client.[12,14] An example of prescribing the symptom is telling an insomniac to try and stay up all night and not sleep for a month. This effectively changes the context from one of trying to sleep (which is not working) to one of trying to stay up. When this, as expected, fails, the objective of sleep is achieved. The result of techniques such as these is that the patient begins to formulate a new world view, to see that the inevitable is *not* inevitable, or that it is ludicrous and not frightening, or that it is something that can be controlled by the person. Bruner gives an example of treating a child's fear of making mistakes in school.[2] During tutoring sessions with the child, he changes the context from one of fear of being reprimanded, to a game in which the child deliberately tries to make mistakes:

The eleven-year old boy . . . said to the tutor that he was afraid to make an error in reading because his teacher yelled at him. The tutor asked whether his teacher yelled very loud, and upon being assured that she did, volunteered that he could yell louder than the teacher, and urged his patient to make a mistake and see. The boy did, and his tutor in mock voice yelled as loud as he could. The boy jumped. Tutor to patient: "Can she yell louder than that?" Patient: "Yes, lots." Tutor: "Make another error and I'll try to get louder still." (p. 482)[2]

The child was eventually able to treat mistakes playfully and to progress with and master his reading lessons.

In families, second-order change may involve relabeling a problem, and thereby shifting it from one individual to the family interaction system, or creating therapeutic double-binds.[3,14,15] The latter means that "the therapist must create situations that force the family into a bind. Either it continues its behavior, but does so under the command of the therapist, or it rebels, thus producing the desired change" (p. 482).[3] In either case, the family sees that its pathological interaction patterns or norms are subject to control and hence, can be changed. For instance, if the family norms consist of the father's setting limits or prescribing punishments while the mother plays the role of peace-maker or mediator, the therapist's interventions might be directed at helping the parents realize that the problem does not lie in the child's infraction of rules or the unfairness of punishments, but in the lack of an alliance between the parents.

Communications/interaction theorists, because of their belief that recurring patterns of behavior dominate family and social interaction, are especially interested in discovering family "rituals." A family ritual is a special pattern of behavior involving the entire family.[12] Eating together every night at 6 p.m. may be a family ritual. Some rituals, however, can be pathogenic or destructive—for instance, a weekly family bridge game in which the father consistently berates his partner. Replacing the pathogenic ritual with a therapeutic ritual is another type of second-order change.[12] Suggesting that the family try a noncompetitive activity instead of the bridge game might lead to the inculcation of a more positive ritual.

Both first-order and second-order changes are relevant to various problems, but to attempt either when the opposite is needed will create an impasse. The communications/interaction group therefore adheres to a problem-solving model of treatment for both individuals and families. This model begins with a concrete and clear specification of the problem. The next step is to determine what behaviors or patterns are maintaining the problem. From this, it is then possible to begin identifying whether first- or second-order change is needed.[14,15] If second-order change is necessary, attempts are made to relabel or re-context behavior, and to change behavior through paradoxical instructions, thera-peutic double-binds, and therapeutic rituals.

CRITICISMS AND LIMITATIONS

One of the initial criticisms of the communications/interaction body of knowledge derives from its use of the "black box" analogy—that the mind can be compared to a black box, whose contents it is *not necessary to see* in order to understand behavior.[13] By not accounting for this unseen inner "structure," however, the role and importance of emotions and cognitions (concepts important to other schools of psychological thought) are minimized, while the importance of interaction as a focus increases.[3] Many critics also liken the theory to behaviorism and accuse its proponents of "a lack of understanding of the basic inner condition of the patient" (p. 134).[11] However, by limiting their domain to the behavioral effects of communication, com-munications/interaction theorists are not denying the existence of emotions, will, or motives; they are merely asserting that behavior can be changed without recourse to these phenomena. And, in fact, they very much believe in the individual's self-control. The ultimate goal of paradoxical treatment strategies is to lead people to seeing that they do have control over what they do.

Another source of criticism concerns the use of the Theory of Logical Types (i.e., different levels of communication) to explain the paradox created in a double-bind situation. One critic stated that "the double bind theory is 'an example of . . . mathematico-logical pseudo-psychologizing'" (p. 135),[11] and another indicated that what is described as levels of communication are more accurately a variety of dimensions, some pertaining to the actual communi-cation while others are more descriptive of the individuals doing the com-munication.[10] Yet, the point of the communications/interaction theorists is that all communication does more than just convey a message; it also says something about the relationship between the people communicating. It is when this latter aspect of the communication is ignored, not correctly under-stood, or contradictory with the intent of the verbal message that pathology arises. Thus, this criticism either reflects an incomplete understanding of the premises of communications/interaction theory, or it must be taken as a rejection of communications/interaction theory as a whole.

The double-bind hypothesis is also criticized for lacking empirical research support. However, there is a plethora of published qualitative studies, tran-scripts, and case histories supporting the hypothesis. The deeper issue appears to be distrust of the qualitative/case *methods* used by the communications/interaction school to support the theory. Given the concerns of this school, extensive use of transcripts, cases, and qualitative data seems an appropriate methodological approach. The theory does not lend itself to experimental, correlational, or other quantitative methods.

This body of knowledge has limited itself to examination of observable phenomena and, in particular, communication. It has not sought to address issues such as motivation or drive-satisfaction, developmental stages, cognition, and a host of other phenomena. In addition, communications/interaction theorists do not accept role theory as being compatible with their views, because roles are seen as oriented toward individuals rather than interactions.[5] Further, these theorists do not comment on the external environment of the family system; although they acknowledge the potential impact of external events, their primary focus is on the family's interactional system.

In sum, criticism of this theory is aimed in part at the limitations of the theory, particularly its avoidance of psychodynamics. Nevertheless, communications/interaction theorists have addressed a prevalent phenomenon—communication—that had hitherto been given little attention, and they have done so in a unique manner.

COMMENTARY

Although this body of knowledge has targeted communication as its focus, some of its implications can enhance understanding of occupational performance and is therefore relevant to occupational therapy.

First, the focus on the family as an interactional system is relevant to understanding how exploration or play might be stifled in a child. In the family where the double-bind is a rule of life, a child might very quickly choose inaction as being safer than exploration. Eventually, the child may begin to avoid action in other settings as well, failing to learn the skills that other children acquire through play and exploration. However, occupational therapists also seek to understand the development of occupational behavior by examination of the adequacy of family members as role models, as well as by an examination of the resources and environment of the family.[7] Therefore, the communications/interaction perspective is only partially useful to an understanding of how pathological families might stifle childhood occupation.

The emphasis of communications/interaction theorists on the way in which ordered behavior reflects the *context* of that behavior is particularly relevant to occupational therapy treatment. A major role of the occupational therapist is the creation of contexts that give meaning to people's behaviors.[6] In other words, when the occupational therapist's goal is to enable someone to develop punctuality, discipline, and other work-appropriate behaviors, he or she tries to create a setting in which these behaviors are natural and expected. Thus, the therapist may involve this person in an assembly-line project, at the same hours every day, rather than in a once-a-week social games group. The latter context, however, might be right for someone needing to explore and experiment with new leisure interests.

Finally, on a practical level, occupational therapists are part of an interactional system with their clients and patients. Familiarity with the ambiguities and potentials of communication and metacommunication can only enhance therapeutic effectiveness and humanity. For instance, the nonverbal communication conveyed by a uniform and clipboard may be contrary to a stated message to a client that the therapist wants to *collaborate* with this person on goal setting. Similarly, the use of manipulative techniques may tell patients that therapists see themselves as authorities, even as they ask patients to share in guiding their own treatment.

In summary, then, the communications/interactional body of knowledge is one which can contribute to understanding the development of disordered occupational performance. At the same time, one must be aware of its limitations and different overall emphasis from that of occupational therapy. We have already incorporated some of its action implications into our own practice, in the form of creating therapeutic contexts; this body of knowledge provides an additional perspective for understanding the importance of doing so. Last, the recognition of how discrepancies between verbal and nonverbal communication may create double-binds for our clients is particularly relevant to understanding ourselves in therapeutic relationships.

SUMMARY

History and Purpose	Dissatisfaction with views of behavior as either exclusively inner-determined or environmentally determined led communications/interaction theorists to seek explanations of behavior in terms of communication patterns in interpersonal relationships.
	Theory is dominated by an interest in understanding peculiar speech patterns of people with schizophrenia.

View of Order	Theory base is derived from four sources: information theory, cybernetics, systems theory, and the theory of logical types.
	Ordered communication is a process of information exchange, in which frequently repeated events come to be recognized as socially expected.
	Behavior is understood in relationship to the context of that behavior; individuals recognize what behaviors are appropriate for different contexts (e.g., church, school, etc.) and are able to shift and manipulate contexts.
	Contexts and nonverbal communication are of a different logical type than the verbal content of communication; nonverbal communication lends meaning to the context.
	Families are open systems that can be characterized by unique communication patterns; these patterns prescribe acceptable, or ordered, behavior for the family.
View of Disorder	Schizophrenia, the primary concern of this school, is the outcome of disordered family communication.
	Disordered communication involves giving contradictory messages to a "victim" (usually the child), and creating a "no-win," "no-escape" situation known as the double-bind.
	The person caught in a double-bind learns to deny his or her perceptions instead of understanding and using metacommunication the same way others do.
	Bizarre schizophrenic behaviors are strategies for dealing with the double-bind.

Action Implications	Two types of change are distinguished: first-order change, which involves decreasing or increasing some behavior already present, and second-order change, which involves relabeling the problem, or placing it in a new context.
	In the family system, second-order change means shifting the problem from the individual to the family interaction system.
	The therapist seeks to uncover pathological interaction patterns and family rituals and to replace them with healthy patterns and rituals.
Criticisms and Limitations	The theory has been criticized for ignoring role of emotions, for use of complicated language and constructs, and for lack of empirical research support.
	Theory is limited to study of communication and does not address issues such as motivation or role theory.
Commentary	Double-bind phenomenon can add to our understanding of how family life might stifle the development of occupational behavior in children.
	Occupational therapy treatment involves the manipulation of contexts to give meaning to the activities of our clients; this theory increases our understanding of how ordered behavior relates to the context of that behavior.
	Therapists and their clients form a communication system; familiarity with ambiguities and potentials of communication and metacommunication can enhance the effectiveness of this communication system.

TERMS AND CONCEPTS

catatonia   in communications/interaction theory, a disorder in which a person attempts to *not* communicate with others.

context   total sum of the human and nonhuman components which comprise the scene in which a behavior occurs; sets the stage for behaviors.

cybernetics   the monitoring/regulation of behavior through the receipt of relevant feedback in order to maintain a predetermined goal or state, e.g., a thermostat.

double-bind   situation in which contradictory messages are conveyed to an individual by another person(s), providing an unclear message for expected behavior. Pathologically, these patterns of interaction occur repeatedly and the individual withdraws from the situation by developing bizarre behavior in response to it.

first-order change   behavioral change accomplished within a given context, generally by increasing or decreasing behaviors that already occur in that context.

hebephrenia   in communications/interaction theory, a disorder in which a person avoids communicating by laughing at all messages.

metacommunication communication about communication; information conveyed through such phenomena as the context of behavior, body language, use of space, clothing, and so on, which gives added meaning to the verbal content of the communication.

open system   an organized complex of parts which dynamically interact in successive cycles of input, throughput, output, and feedback, in order to accomplish some purpose or goal in a coherent fashion.

paranoia   in communications/interaction theory, a disorder of communication in which a person continually searches for hidden meanings in what others say.

paradox
situation in which individual is instructed to behave in what seems to be a contradictory or absurd manner in order to precipitate new ways of thinking about the situation. As a treatment technique, it is a form of bringing about second-order change.

second-order change
behavioral change accomplished through reconceptualization of the context in which the behavior occurs. Therapeutically this may be achieved by using paradoxical instructions, therapeutic double-binds, and/or therapeutic rituals.

REFERENCES

1. Bateson, G., Jackson, D. D., Haley, J., & Weakland, J. H. Toward a theory of schizophrenia. In G. Bateson (Ed.), *Steps to an ecology of mind*. San Francisco: Chandler, 1972.
2. Bruner, J. S. On coping and defending. In J. Coleman (Ed.), *The psychology of effective behavior*. Glenview, Ill.: Scott, Foresman, 1969.
3. Foley, V. D. Family therapy. In R. J. Corsini (Ed.), *Current psychotherapies* (2nd ed.). Itasca, Ill.: Peacock, 1979.
4. Henley, N. M. *Body politics: Power, sex, and nonverbal communication*. Englewood Cliffs, N.J.: Prentice-Hall, 1977.
5. Jackson, D. D. The study of the family. In P. Watzlawick & J. H. Weakland (Eds.), *The interactional view*. New York: Norton, 1977.
6. Kielhofner, G. The art of occupational therapy. In G. Kielhofner (Ed.), *Health through occupation: Theory and practice in occupational therapy*. Philadelphia: F. A. Davis, 1983.
7. de Renne-Stephan, C. Imitation: A mechanism of play behavior. *American Journal of Occupational Therapy*, 1980, *34*, 95–102.
8. Ruesch, J., & Kees, W. *Nonverbal communication*. Berkeley: University of California, 1969.
9. Scheflen, A. E. *Body language and social order*. Englewood Cliffs, N.J.: Prentice-Hall, 1972.
10. Schuham, A. I. The double-bind hypothesis: A decade later. *Psychological Bulletin*, 1967, *68*, 409–416.
11. Watzlawick, P. A review of the double-bind theory. *Family Process*, 1963, *2*, 132–152.
12. Watzlawick, P. *The language of change*. New York: Basic Books, 1978.
13. Watzlawick, P., Beavin, J. H., & Jackson, D. D. *Pragmatics of human communication*. New York: Norton, 1967.

14. Watzlawick, P., Weakland, J. H., & Fisch, R. *Change: Principles of problem formation and problem resolution.* New York: Norton, 1974.
15. Weakland, J. H., Fisch, R., Watzlawick, P., & Bodin, A. M. Brief therapy: Focused problem resolution. In P. Watzlawick & J. H. Weakland (Eds.), *The interactional view.* New York: Norton, 1977.

ADDITIONAL READINGS

Ruesch, J., & Bateson, G. *Communication: The social matrix of psychiatry.* New York: Norton, 1951.

Weakland, J. H. The "double-bind" hypothesis of schizophrenia and three-party interaction. In D. D. Jackson (Ed.), *The etiology of schizophrenia.* New York: Basic Books, 1960.

Swenson, C. H. *Introduction to interpersonal relations.* Glenview, Ill.: Scott, Foresman, 1973.

9

Social Ecological Approaches

Approaches to psychosocial practice that emphasize the role of the environment, or milieu, in promoting health, can be grouped together under the rubric of social ecology. Included among these approaches are the therapeutic community, milieu therapy, and ecological psychology. Despite their common orientation to the environment as a critical dimension of health, these approaches are not a unified body of knowledge, and the reader would probably not find them grouped together in this way in other literature. Nevertheless, they share a fundamental difference from somatic or psychotherapeutic approaches to mental illness—their focus on the environment or context of treatment.[2] This chapter presents an amalgamation of these approaches in order to provide a perspective for understanding the contributions occupational therapists can make to the therapeutic use of the environment.

Some initial definitions will clarify the scope of this body of knowledge. Cummings[5] identifies the therapeutic community and milieu therapy as being two major approaches to the use of the environment in therapy. Traditionally, the therapeutic community designated an environment that focused on helping patients achieve insight and emotional control. As such, the social environment, or the roles of staff and patients, was the primary environmental concern, and various forms of therapy were incorporated into the therapeutic community as different means to the same end.[5] The therapeutic community was typically characterized by community meetings and an emphasis on achieving *insight* into one's problems or difficulties in interpersonal situations. Milieu therapy referred to a therapeutic environment that was organized around the goal of helping patients improve their competence in problem-solving and daily-living skills. Different therapies were incorporated into this context for their relevance to ordinary life and for their potential to present the patient with practical problems to solve.[5] Milieu therapy would thus be characterized by assigned tasks and chores for community maintenance, groups pertaining to the development of self-care skills, and an attempt to approximate the demands of the outside world.

The distinction represented by these terms is somewhat lost in present-day psychosocial settings. In some instances, writers use the terms therapeutic community and milieu therapy interchangeably; however, others continue to use them to evoke distinctly different philosophies with accordingly different implications for treatment. The therapeutic community and milieu therapy, however, address the therapeutic potential of the treatment setting. In contrast to this, ecological psychology addresses person-environment interactions in *any* setting. Ecological psychology, with its more global perspective, enables a deeper understanding of how the treatment environment can be a beneficial or destructive setting for patients.[21]

The view presented in this chapter is that these approaches naturally complement one another and can be examined together. Once the environment is acknowledged as having an impact on therapy, any treatment setting and its inhabitants can become the subject of examination. Thus, the target population of the various environmental therapies is not limited to a specific diagnostic or age group or a specific locale. Therapeutic communities and milieu therapy programs have been used in prisons, drug rehabilitation settings, and psychiatric hospitals and with children and adults of all ages.

HISTORY AND PURPOSE

Advocates of moral treatment in the late eighteenth and early nineteenth centuries believed that mental illness was directly related to the environment and that, consequently, the role of the psychiatric institution was to provide a milieu in which patients would demonstrate desirable behavior.[26] Concern with the environment was overshadowed in the nineteenth century by the rapid growth of institutions and the rise of the medical organic explanation of mental illness, leading to an increasingly custodial approach to care and the use of whatever somatic and physical therapies were currently popular.[11,19,26]

Psychoanalysis and the two World Wars caused another reconceptualization of theories of mental illness and treatment. In particular, World War I sensitized psychiatrists to an awareness of the relationship between the social environment and mental illness.[19] This growing awareness of the role of the social environment led Sullivan and Menninger, two psychoanalysts with an interpersonal perspective, to begin to deliberately structure the social environment of psychiatric wards as a therapeutic tool, and to explicitly emphasize the therapeutic role of ward personnel.[26]

In the 1950s, the writings of various anthropologists, sociologists, and novelists greatly enhanced the awareness of the connections between patients' behavior, staff interpersonal relationships, and other aspects of the treatment environment (see Additional Readings). At the same time, neo-Freudians (see Chapter 3) and ego psychologists were expanding on Freud's notions of personality development to emphasize the influence of sociocultural contexts on development.[26]

Two landmarks in the development of environmental approaches to therapy were the work of Maxwell Jones, who developed and wrote about therapeutic communities in England,[8] and the work of Cumming and Cumming,[6] whose ideas represented a synthesis and advancement of environmental trends and the new ego psychologies. Recently, ecological and environmental psychologists have added to this body of knowledge by examining the impact of physical factors in the environment—such as lighting, room size, furniture arrangements, and staff-patient ratios—and of the psychosocial atmosphere on patients' behavior, discharge rates, recidivism, and so on.[8,14,16,20,26]

This tradition has been developed by humanitarians, anthropologists, psychoanalysts, social workers, psychologists, and social scientists. It views the social and physical environment as being intimately linked with the behavior of people. It differs from behaviorism in that it does not see the individual as a passive respondent to the environment, and it differs from organic and classic intrapsychic models of mental health in that it does not see the environment as irrelevant to the development of the individual, or locate the cause of disorder primarily within the patient.

VIEW OF ORDER

For those writers who see the therapeutic community only as a context for organizing a variety of treatments, no particular theory base or view of order is espoused. However, writers whose focus is on person-environment interactions, in treatment or other settings, do present a distinct theory and perspective on order. This latter approach, exemplified by the work of the Cummings[6] and of various ecological psychologists, forms the basis of this discussion.

The Cummings pull together a variety of concepts from ego psychology, sociology, and cognitive psychology to present a theory of human development that focuses on the ego and the environment. They begin by conceptualizing the ego as being an affective and cognitive structure that enables the person to meet and respond to the environment. The ego contains certain capacities, such as thought, perception, and the capacity for motor development, that are latent until the right conditions present themselves. These latent capacities represent potentials for responding to future events. When propitious circumstances or developmental crises arise, the ego will synthesize these capacities in order to enable the individual to accommodate to the milieu and to influence it.[6]

Another major concept in the Cummings' theory is that of differentiation. This term is used to refer to two processes. First, the individual occupies a life space that becomes increasingly differentiated, complex, and integrated as the person explores the environment, grows, and learns. Second, the ego as well becomes differentiated throughout the process of interacting with the environment. The growing child begins to organize objects, ideas, events, and values into sets of relationships, or ego sets. These sets might group together feelings and events that the child has come to associate with one another, such as a warm, loving feeling associated with birthday parties. Or they might categorize classes of objects that share common features, such as female adults. Through the acquisition and organization of these sets, the child learns to discriminate between aspects or qualities of an object, and to generalize aspects to other situations.[6] For instance, a little girl might form a set consisting of female adults. From this set she may learn that although teachers and mothers are similar in their tendency to be caring and nurturing, the teacher's concern is limited to behavior and work in school, while a mother's is more apt to include interest in her friends, eating and sleeping habits, and clothes.

Throughout development, losses and additions of sets require reorganization of the ego, to tie up loose ends and replace meanings that are no longer valid. This process of organizing and reorganizing the ego thus requires a certain stability and predictability in the environment. However, too few stimuli and too little variety in the environment might result in an inadequately organized ego and an inability to deal with changes. The environment, therefore, contributes to the process of development through the opportunities, diversity, fluctuations, and organization inherent within it.[6] As a result of this interactive process, the degree of organization and differentiation of the ego and the degree of ambiguity and richness in the environment come to be reflected in a range of responses in the individual, from curiosity and learning to anxiety and incompetence. The Cummings therefore conclude that ego growth, or the development of psychosocial order, reflects an ongoing process of encountering new opportunities in the environment; reorganizing one's responses, associated meanings and feelings to accommodate these new opportunities; and then meeting the environment again (which now appears different, due to the individual's learning) with these changed perceptions.

This view of order in psychological development is compatible with ecological psychologists' view of development as a process of becoming effective in an increasing range of increasingly complex settings.[4] In fact, the emphasis of ecological psychology on overt interrelationships between people and settings clarifies and completes the Cummings' discussion of order.

To begin with, ecological psychology conceives of the physical milieu in dynamic terms. Physical settings both promote certain patterns of behavior and can be recognized by these characteristic behavior patterns. Nevertheless, these settings are dynamic, open systems, characterized simultaneously by change and stability. They may be changed by the actions of individuals or by natural events, and such changes may occur in the physical or social aspects of the setting. When a setting changes so that it is no longer conducive to the behavior originally associated with it, that behavior may reappear in another setting. Finally, settings are continually exerting influence on inhabitants' behavior, whether or not the inhabitants perceive this to be happening.[22] Human order as described in these propositions is a process of recognizing what behaviors are expected in various settings, determining which settings are appropriate for one's goals, performing in a variety of settings, and appropriately adapting settings to meet changing needs.

Taken together, there is a core of beliefs that relate behavior to the physical and social environment in a dynamic, mutually influential process. From the Cummings' view of ego development we obtain the picture of a person who brings certain characteristics and potentials for functioning and learning in various settings. From ecological psychology, we see that environments present and can be organized to provide individuals with options for further learning and growth. As individuals purposefully engage in these settings, they develop acceptable social behavior, learn to exert influence on settings, and organize and reorganize their capacities, values, and feelings for future interactions with the environment.

VIEW OF DISORDER

A parallel view of disorder in this tradition again has two focuses: disorder in terms of ego psychology, and disorder in terms of person/environment interactions. The Cummings delineate four types of pathology. The first is ego poverty, or too few organizational sets in the ego. Ego poverty might result from an environmentally deprived childhood or from the loss of ego sets due to trauma of some sort. A person with too few ego sets would be unable to deal with complex situations, might respond to all situations with one modal response, or might invent inappropriate mechanisms for dealing with the environment. A second type of pathology arises from poor differentiation of ego sets. In this case, because the sets do not clearly identify or classify situations, the individual would not be able to choose the right set for dealing with a particular event. An example might be a person who feels that clothing is the key to his or her identity and therefore dresses in the same way for all occasions. Another form of pathology occurs when the ego sets are not organized in terms of a hierarchy that would enable the person to determine which responses are appropriate for the present and which should be retained for the future. The epitome of this is the person who feels that everything must be changed now and is unable to identify the realistic changes that can be made in the immediate present and those that should be saved for the future. Finally, ego disorganization may arise from severe environmental stress. Although the ego may have organized, differentiated sets, under certain disastrous conditions the individual may be too aroused to draw on them in a meaningful way.[6]

Implicit in this discussion of disorder is the sense that functional behavior is contingent on the individual's having enough previous experiences in different settings to be able to select the most adaptive response to the current setting. The potential in this interaction for the occurrence of maladaptive behavior is made more explicit by ecological psychologists. Their perspective closely parallels that of ego psychology, but they emphasize the importance of the environment, rather than the development of an intrapsychic structure (i.e., the ego). For instance, the individual whose development has been limited to settings that stress highly similar behavior patterns would be ill-equipped to perform and solve problems under novel conditions because he or she has not had opportunities to experience unpredictable or unfamiliar environments. Or the person who is unable to discriminate the different behaviors demanded by various settings might perform inappropriately in settings, or seek out settings unsuited to accomplishing goals. Because people with a wider range of behaviors, experiences, and competencies can more easily adapt to a wide range of settings, disordered behavior becomes a cyclical response in which the individual, lacking competence, avoids or fails in new experiences, making it less likely that the behavioral flexibility necessary to competence will develop.[18]

ACTION IMPLICATIONS

The action implications of the social ecological approaches fall into two groups: (1) strategies primarily concerned with restructuring the social environment so that all interpersonal encounters have therapeutic value; and (2) strategies for redesigning the physical and task environments to communicate expectations for socially competent behavior. Potentially the two approaches can converge in terms of community norms or expectations for behavior.

A critical aspect of the social environment is the role of the patient. Endemic to the creation of a therapeutic environment is the process of "relabeling" the patient from a sick and passive recipient of care to an active community member, capable of assuming responsibility.[2] In the therapeutic milieu the patient is viewed as a responsible manager of his or her affairs.[6] Along with redefinition of the patient role, staff roles are necessarily redefined as well. Thus, decision making and authority are rationally delegated to different community members.[2,6,17] This creates the opportunity for role paralleling, in which the more competent community members—staff and patients—serve as role models for the less competent.[2]

Another social strategy is that of limit setting and containment. These terms refer to the control or limiting of symptomatic behavior so that therapy can progress.[1,12] Behaviors that would be the focus of limit setting are destructiveness, autistic or regressed behaviors, acting out, extreme dependency, and withdrawal from the environment.[1]

The last major social strategy is that of attention saturation or involvement. This strategy consists of the intensive use of social activities that direct the patient's attention away from inner preoccupations and toward the social community.[2,12] Techniques such as intense social contact, ritual activities, and peer pressure are used to communicate this message.[2]

The second group of strategies involves changing expectations for behavior through changes in the task and physical environments. First, the environment must be one in which the patient can orient him- or herself and feel safe enough to investigate and perhaps try out new behaviors.[6] This is achieved through providing continuity with the patient's previous and future environments; using clear, concrete markings to enable the patient to geographically locate him- or herself; identifying staff with name tags; reinforcing the patient's self-identification by allowing access to mirrors, grooming implements, personal artifacts, and street clothes; and orienting patients to time, with clocks and calendars.[6] Similarly, the environment must reduce fears for personal welfare and security through such means as adequate heating and lighting, comfortable sleeping quarters, and tasteful food.[21]

Traditional assumptions about the physical design of treatment environments are also targeted for examination by this strategy. For instance, the traditional assumption that patients should not be alone has been countered by research showing that lack of privacy in patients' bedrooms may actually lead to an increase in passive, isolated behavior,[15] which would not enhance the patient's social involvement or orientation to the overall environment. Similarly, certain furniture arrangements may induce the same isolated behaviors.[14] Thus, opportunities for choice and flexibility in the environment have become increasingly important in treatment settings.

The other major component of this group of interventions is the provision of opportunities for learning and practicing productive behavior.[1,2,6,17] Transforming the environment into a problem-solving arena implies continuity and overlap of the treatment setting with problems and expectations of the external environment. In this sense, the therapeutic environment can be considered a "school for living," in which the coursework consists of situations that parallel the demands of ordinary life.[17] Task expectations for patients therefore range from involvement in ward management to productive occupation and recreation.[6,8]

Ultimately, both groups of strategies merge in the creation of norms and values pertaining to the uniqueness of the community.[2] These values are maintained by the community and serve to inculcate newcomers to its expectations. Mechanisms such as community meetings, support and reinforcement of valued behaviors, and communication networks of individuals help to create and transmit the shared norms and total environmental demands for socially productive behavior.

CRITICISMS AND LIMITATIONS

Criticisms are generally made in reference to therapeutic communities and milieu therapy, and not to the more recent ecological approaches. First, the ambiguity and inconsistency in defining terms cause professionals to have differing expectations and understandings of this tradition. The lack of one conceptual model underlying the therapeutic community or milieu therapy has meant that professionals who support these approaches are more apt to share with one another perceptions of what they are opposed to than what they favor.[3,24] Further, the eclecticism of the framework has contributed to an eclecticism of treatment techniques in some instances; in other instances, there is a tendency to latch on to the more immediately recognizable trappings of a therapeutic community (e.g., community meetings) without truly incorporating the goals that should characterize a therapeutic environment.[5]

The second group of criticisms derives from the changed role definitions of staff and patients. The leveling of hierarchy and concomitant role blurring among staff often create confusion, tension, and dissatisfaction for many staff who may feel that they are not prepared for their new roles and that they are not using skills they have.[13,17] In addition, although one of the basic assumptions of milieu strategies is that patients should take on greater responsibility, in reality their role may continue to be as restricted as it was in a medical or other model of treatment.[25]

Third, criticisms have been levied against milieu therapy and therapeutic communities with regard to their effectiveness. Therapeutic communities, because of the emphasis on involvement in community life, tend to prolong the patient's stay rather than returning the patient to the outside community.[13] However, expediency in discharge has not been linked to tenure in the external community,[8] so this is not an unequivocal criticism. Related to effectiveness is the charge that behaviors valued in the therapeutic milieu may differ from behaviors valued outside of it. For instance, speaking one's mind or sharing anxieties may be appropriate in the hospital but inappropriate at work.[17] Further, there has been a tendency to assume that therapeutic communities and milieu strategies are equally effective for all types of patients.[13] However, because many therapeutic communities are more talk-oriented than activity-oriented, their effectiveness may be limited to an elite population of highly verbal patients. Finally, because of the variations in implementation of therapeutic communities, research and program evaluation is difficult to carry out and difficult to use as a basis for generalization to other programs.[5,17]

COMMENTARY

In the 1960s Reilly described a model occupational therapy program as a total milieu or culture

> which acknowledges competency, arouses curiosity, feeds in universal knowledge, deepens appreciations and demands behavior across the full spectrum of a human's abilities. . . . It presses for the exercising of life skills in a balanced pattern of daily living. (pp. 63–64)[23]

This prescription was virtually a criticism of the fact that milieu therapy and therapeutic communities had become settings where patients and staff sat and talked about problems, smoked cigarettes, and drank coffee, but engaged in no other activity. These were "under-arousing" environments, posing no challenges to the patient. Because the therapeutic community and milieu therapy had deviated from their original conceptions, Reilly felt that there was no place for occupational therapy in such a setting.

Occupational therapy, however, has traditionally espoused the values presumably held by the milieu movement. Early journals of occupational therapy abound with examples of programs in which the occupational therapy department was responsible for directing recreational programs, industrial activities, personal hygiene and beauty care classes, exercise and dance classes, and hobby shops; arranging trips to local community facilities; and planning and supervising informal socialization and leisure.[9] In addition, an awareness of the need for understanding the interrelationships between the physical and psychosocial environments and occupational performance has permeated the writing of occupational therapists.[7,10,16] Because of these long-held beliefs and practices, occupational therapy is well suited for a leadership role in designing and implementing therapeutic environments.

SUMMARY

History and Purpose	Social ecological approaches have their roots in moral treatment.
	World Wars resensitized psychiatrists to social environmental factors in mental illness.
	Sullivan and Menninger were early proponents of structuring ward social environments.
	Jones developed therapeutic communities in England. Cumming and Cumming synthesized ego psychology and environmental approaches.
	A current growing research tradition in ecological psychology has increased understanding of person-environment interactions.
	The tradition as a whole seeks to understand the potential of the environment as a therapeutic tool.
View of Order	*Ego psychology:*
	Individuals organize patterns of events into sets within ego. These sets enable discrimination between and generalization to future events.
	Development requires continual reorganization of the ego.
	Variety and opportunities in the environment contribute to organization of the ego.
	Ecological psychology:
	Development involves learning to be competent in a variety of settings.
	Settings promote certain behaviors and are subject to change by their inhabitants. Individuals learn to choose settings that are appropriate to their goals and to modify settings.
	Through purposeful engagement in settings, the individual develops acceptable social behavior.

View of Disorder	*Ego psychology:*
	Disorder occurs because the individual with a poorly organized ego cannot respond appropriately to the environment.
	Ecological psychology:
	A lack of experience in varied settings may lead to a lack of behavioral flexibility for functioning in a wide range of environments.
	The individual may choose inappropriate settings for goal attainment or may not know what behaviors are required by the setting.
Action Implications	Restructuring the social environment involves:
	—relabeling "patient" as "member."
	—limit setting on symptomatic behavior.
	—attention saturation.
	—role paralleling.
	Redesigning the physical and task environments includes:
	—orienting the patient to self and surroundings.
	—reassessment of traditional physical design assumptions.
	—opportunities for problem solving and practice of productive behavior.

Criticisms and Limitations	Because of the lack of one clear conceptual model, definitions are ambiguous and inconsistent.
	Practice is often marked by an eclecticism of techniques.
	Role blurring often leads to role strain.
	Excessive emphasis on talk at the expense of action has predominated, making appropriateness dubious for all but the highly verbal.
	Because of program variations, it is difficult to evaluate effectiveness of therapeutic communities in general.
Commentary	Occupational therapy has traditionally held beliefs associated with the milieu movement.
	Disintegration of milieu into a talk environment has meant that occupational therapy has become incompatible with milieu/therapeutic community.
	An awareness of the relationship between occupational performance and the environment and traditional moral treatment values have prepared occupational therapists to assume a leadership role as environmental managers.

TERMS AND CONCEPTS

attention saturation	the intensive use of social activities to direct a patient's attention toward the social environment and away from preoccupations with inner problems.
containment	limit setting on symptomatic behaviors such as acting out.
ego poverty	the existence of too few ego sets, resulting from environmental deprivation, lack of experience, or trauma.
ego set	the organization of objects, ideas, events, and values into a meaningful pattern of relationships.

milieu therapy	a therapeutic environment designed to help patients improve their competence in problem solving and daily living skills.
modal response	the use of one form of behavior to deal with many different situations.
role paralleling	the use of more competent community members as role models for the less competent.
therapeutic community	an environment that uses all staff, patients, and a variety of treatment techniques to help patients achieve insight and emotional control.

REFERENCES

1. Abroms, G. M. Defining milieu therapy. *Archives of General Psychiatry*, 1969, *21*, 553–560.
2. Almond, R. Issues in milieu treatment. *Schizophrenia Bulletin*, Summer 1975, 12–26.
3. Armor, D. J., & Klerman, G. L. Psychiatric treatment orientations and professional ideology. *Journal of Health and Social Behavior*, 1968, 9, 243–255.
4. Bronfenbrenner, U. *The ecology of human development: Experiments by nature and design*. Cambridge: Harvard University Press, 1979.
5. Cumming, E. "Therapeutic community" and "milieu therapy" strategies can be distinguished. *International Journal of Psychiatry*, 1969, 7, 204–208.
6. Cumming, J., & Cumming, E. *Ego and milieu: Theory and practice of environmental therapy*. New York: Atherton, 1967.
7. Dunning, H. Environmental occupational therapy. *American Journal of Occupational Therapy*, 1972, 26, 292–298.
8. Ellsworth, R., Maroney, R., Klett, W., Gordon, H., & Gunn, R. Milieu characteristics of successful psychiatric treatment programs. *American Journal of Orthopsychiatry*, 1971, *41*, 427–441.
9. Feuss, C. D., Jr., & Maltby, J. W. Occupational therapy in the therapeutic community. *American Journal of Occupational Therapy*, 1959, *13*, 9–10, 25.
10. Gray, M. Effects of hospitalization on work-play behavior. *American Journal of Occupational Therapy*, 1972, 26, 180–185.
11. Grob, G. N. *Mental institutions in America: Social policy to 1875*. New York: Free Press, 1973.

12. Gunderson, J. G. Defining the therapeutic processes in psychiatric milieus. *Psychiatry*, 1978, *41*, 327–335.
13. Herz, M. I. The therapeutic community: A critique. *Hospital and Community Psychiatry*, 1972, *23*, 17–20.
14. Holahan, C. J. Environmental psychology in psychiatric hospital settings. In D. Canter & S. Canter (Eds.), *Designing for therapeutic environments: A review of research*. New York: Wiley, 1979.
15. Ittelson, W. H., Proshansky, H. M., & Rivlin, L. G. The environmental psychology of the psychiatric ward. In H. M. Proshansky, W. H. Ittelson, & L. G. Rivlin (Eds.), *Environmental psychology: Man and his physical setting*. New York: Holt, Rinehart & Winston, 1970.
16. Kannegieter, R. B. Environmental interactions in occupational therapy—Some inferences. *American Journal of Occupational Therapy*, 1980, *34*, 715–720.
17. Kraft, A. The therapeutic community. In A. Dean, A. M. Kraft, & B. Pepper (Eds.), *The social setting of mental health*. New York: Basic Books, 1976.
18. Lawton, M. P. *Environment and aging*. Monterey: Brooks/Cole, 1980.
19. Magaro, P., Gripp, R., McDowell, D. J., & Miller, I. W., III. *The mental health industry: A cultural phenomenon*. New York: Wiley, 1978.
20. Moos, R. H. *Evaluating treatment environments: A social ecological approach*. New York: Wiley, 1974.
21. Peterson, C. R. The challenge of the therapeutic milieu in light of human ecology. *Provo Papers*, Winter 1966–67, 11–50.
22. Proshansky, H. M., Ittelson, W. H., & Rivlin, L. G. The influence of the environment on behavior: Some basic assumptions. In H. M. Proshansky, W. H. Ittelson, & L. G. Rivlin (Eds.), *Environmental psychology: Man and his physical setting*. New York: Holt, Rinehart & Winston, 1970.
23. Reilly, M. A psychiatric occupational therapy program as a teaching model. *American Journal of Occupational Therapy*, 1966, *22*, 61–67.
24. Strauss, A., Schatzman, L., Bucher, R., Ehrlich, D., & Sabshin, M. *Psychiatric ideologies and institutions*. London: Collier-Macmillan, 1964.
25. Wilensky, H., & Herzog, M. I. Problem areas in the development of a therapeutic community. *International Journal of Social Psychiatry*, 1966, *22*, 299–308.
26. Wolf, M. S. A review of literature on milieu therapy. *Journal of Psychiatric Nursing and Mental Health Services*, May 1977, 26–33.

ADDITIONAL READINGS

Caudill, W. *The psychiatric hospital as a small society*. Cambridge: Harvard University Press, 1958.

Goffman, E. *Asylums: Essays on the social situation of mental patients and other inmates.* Garden City, N.Y.: Doubleday, 1961.

Gratke, B. E., & Lux, P. A. Psychiatric occupational therapy in a milieu setting. *American Journal of Occupational Therapy*, 1960, *14*, 13–17.

Holahan, C. J., & Saegert, S. Behavioral and attitudinal effects of large-scale variation in the physical environment of psychiatric wards. *Journal of Abnormal Psychology*, 1973, *82*, 454–462.

Jones, M. *The therapeutic community: A new treatment method in psychiatry.* New York: Basic Books, 1953.

Jones, M. *Social psychiatry in the community, in hospitals, and in prisons.* Springfield, Ill.: Charles C Thomas, 1962.

Noshpitz, J. Milieu therapy. *American Journal of Occupational Therapy*, 1960, *14*, 221–222.

Paul, G. L., & Lentz, R. J. *Psychosocial treatment of chronic mental patients: Milieu versus social-learning programs.* Cambridge: Harvard University Press, 1978.

Stanton, A., & Schwartz, M. *The mental hospital.* New York: Basic Books, 1954.

Toch, H. (Ed.). *Therapeutic communities in corrections.* New York: Praeger, 1980.

Ward, M. J. *The snake pit.* New York: Random House, 1946.

10

Community Mental Health

Community mental health is less a distinct body of knowledge than it is a political movement and a commitment to certain beliefs. As a commitment, it reflects a clear dissatisfaction with certain features of more traditional mental health delivery systems, as well as a belief in several alternatives to these features. As a movement with political origins, it has been embraced by psychiatrists, psychologists, social workers, public health scientists, occupational therapists, nurses, and various community special interest groups that are involved in mental health advocacy programs.

Each major characteristic of community mental health arose in reaction to a dominant characteristic of traditional psychiatric practice.[4] In response to the traditional removal of the individual from the home community to a distant institution, community mental health emphasizes service delivery in the community setting. A traditional lack of concern with the population as a whole has led the movement to identify as its target of treatment or change the community and not the individual. In addition, community mental health has sought to emphasize preventive services instead of curative treatment directed at the reduction of pathology in the individual patient. In an effort to correct the lack of systematic organization and social agency liaisons, the community mental health approach emphasizes continuity and comprehensiveness of care, and service to specific social systems—such as particular geographic regions (catchment areas), schools, or other organizations—developed within the context of a community needs assessment process. Belief in the inadequacy of traditional long-term treatment strategies has led to a focus on innovative techniques such as brief psychotherapy and crisis intervention. To circumvent an impending shortage of traditionally trained personnel, community mental health has looked for ways to use paraprofessional and indigenous mental health workers. Finally, despite varying conceptions of etiology, there is a shared belief that the client cannot be viewed as the sole locus of psychosocial disorder and that community stress may ultimately be the most important factor contributing to psychopathology.[4]

Despite these common themes, however, the movement lacks a cohesive theoretical framework. Panzetta[19] suggests that community mental health can be seen as an *action model*, that is, an approach to the treatment of mental illness that has not been preceded by a fully developed *causal model*, or conceptualization of the formation of mental illness. Hence, the movement is characterized by a plethora of techniques and beliefs about service delivery, rather than by a consistent view of psychosocial order and disorder.

Because of the profusion and confusion of theories that have been brought to the movement by its different adherents, the theory base may appear tenuous. This chapter does not necessarily portray the viewpoints of the entire spectrum of community mental health but represents instead the points of view of prominent writers. Even more important, these views represent the ideals of community mental health and not necessarily the realities.

HISTORY AND PURPOSE

Psychosocial treatment in the late nineteenth century was characterized by two trends: a rapid increase in institutional size, and a changing view of disorder that hypothesized organic rather than environmental causes of mental illness. Because medicine did not possess cures for organically based psychosocial disorders, the combined effect of these two trends was that treatment became largely custodial in nature.[10,16] In the early twentieth century, reformers such as Adoph Meyer and Clifford Beers reacted to this trend by promoting a "citizen's mental hygiene" movement.[4,27] They proposed the establishment of community mental hygiene districts, containing aftercare clinics for follow-up treatment of psychiatric clients, and child guidance clinics, for preventive work with families. Although this movement was overshadowed by the rise of psychoanalysis, the field of psychiatric social work emerged from it.[27]

The mental hygiene movement also foreshadowed a growing awareness of the importance of prevention in mental health. Erikson and Lindemann, both psychologists, had begun to conceptualize psychosocial order as the ability to resolve developmental crises or problems. They postulated that disorder might be prevented in certain individuals if they were helped to acquire coping and problem-solving skills before they were actually faced with particular crises. Following this line of reasoning, Lindemann established a clinic for at-risk populations devoted to preventive techniques and crisis intervention. In his community mental health laboratory, he worked with people facing bereavement and loss, as well as with groups anticipating stressful experiences.[27]

In the 1950s the advent of biochemical treatment for mental illness led to the discharge of large numbers of chronically ill individuals from institutions. At the same time, individual psychotherapy, the form of treatment that had dominated much of the twentieth century, came under substantial attack for lacking effectiveness, social utility, and value.[11]

Finally, the event that most immediately impelled the community mental health movement into existence was the report of a national mental health study, initiated in 1955 and completed in 1961. This report, entitled "Action for Mental Health," recommended that: (1) immediate and intensive care services be provided for acutely psychotic people in outpatient clinics and psychiatric units in general hospitals; (2) that inpatient and outpatient care for chronically mentally ill people be improved; and (3) that public mental health education be implemented to change attitudes toward mental illness.[4] In response to this report, President Kennedy in 1963 proposed a national mental health program, the core of which was the Community Mental Health Centers Act. This act mandated the initial provision of inpatient care, outpatient care, and emergency and education services at community mental health centers. Other services that were eventually required included diagnostic services, rehabilitation, precare and aftercare programs, staff training, and research and evaluation.[4]

VIEW OF ORDER

The community mental health movement does not have a well-articulated view of order. The movement has generally incorporated theories and beliefs from several fields (e.g., social psychology, anthropology, sociology, and environmental psychology) in order to understand psychosocial order and disorder as a social phenomenon.[1] Some of these beliefs delineate a political and psychological view of people and relationships, while others describe a rationale for action implications.

Proponents of community mental health believe that order and disorder are defined by society and culture and that the environment can promote both health and illness.[28] Within this sociocultural environment, interpersonal relationships play a particularly vital role. Community mental health practitioners consider long-term relationships, such as those found within the family, to be a valuable and essential component of psychosocial order.[28]

Theoretically, the cornerstone of the community mental health view of order is a competence, as opposed to a deficit, view of health.[11,26] The competence model is essentially an expansion of the idea that health is the outcome of successful adaptation to the environment.[7] It posits that people have two basic needs: (1) to avoid or adjust to traumatic events, and (2) to engage in positive experiences in order to derive a sense of competence and well-being.

What this suggests is that the disruptive stress of life events can be mitigated when a person evaluates these events positively. Because of the need to feel competence and well-being, people will seek the skills that enable them to successfully cope with stress, in other words, to achieve or maintain mental health.[26]

Because health is viewed in relationship to the environment, the community mental health movement to a large degree shares its theory base with the social ecological approaches (see Chapter 9). In fact, it is reasonable to depict this movement as an extension of therapeutic community/milieu therapy concepts to the larger community outside the institution or treatment setting.

While the theory base of community mental health is not clearly defined, the core of the movement's view of human order is the individual's ability to positively and meaningfully adapt to life events and the environment. For most community mental health workers, the concept of adaptation to the environment implicitly connotes an ability to develop skills and resources to competently interact with the setting, as well as an ability to recognize when the environment needs changing. This view of health stresses the importance of identifying social support systems that maintain or promote health.

VIEW OF DISORDER

The community mental health view of disorder is largely a multifactorial perspective in that it assumes that many factors—genetic, constitutional, developmental, and environmental—contribute differentially to pathology.[11] This model, however, lends itself more to identifying risk factors than to describing disordered behavior.

A major target of the model is the prevailing social structure. Various writers point to the dehumanization that accrues from our consumer-oriented industrial society as being a major risk factor. Excessive industrialization is seen as leading to the dehumanization of work and the loss of a sense of personal identity and competence.[2] These writers contend that present-day community life has contributed to a prevalent feeling of helplessness, leading in turn to alienation and anomie (a feeling of not belonging to society), a lack of faith and trust in service delivery systems, a feeling of lack of control, and the loss of a psychological sense of community.[9]

The social structure also poses risk through its unequal valuation of roles. Certain roles are less valued by society than others, and people in these roles are candidates for psychological problems.[9] This can be further complicated when people fill two or more incompatible roles, or when the roles valued by the whole society conflict with those valued by a subculture.[9] For example, many college students in the early seventies faced a conflict between the alternative, nontraditional life-styles valued by the student subculture and the competitive, economically oriented life-styles valued by their parents and the cultural mainstream.

In addition to the social environment, the physical environment is also considered to be a source of potential stress or risk. Crowding, noise, the fast urban pace of life, and poor lighting conditions are among the many facets of the environment that have been implicated. For instance, crowding has been associated with such deleterious effects as an inability to maintain social relationships, increased aggression, unwillingness to help others, and learned helplessness.[21]

Genetic and organic factors and individual levels of competence are also seen as contributing to disorder. Both order and disorder can therefore be seen as arising from a relationship between organic causes of illness, stressful factors in the environment, individual competence and belief in this competence, and the prevalence and adequacy of social support systems.[2] The ultimate importance of this view lies in its implication that preventing or alleviating stress and improving social support systems will affect a larger number of people and do more to decrease the incidence of mental illness than will the medical emphasis on isolating and treating organic causes.

ACTION IMPLICATIONS

As suggested earlier, community mental health has been more of an action model than a causal or explanatory model. As such, it has led to a variety of interventions, including the development of clubhouse programs for discharged clients; the establishment of short-term, acute care psychiatric units in local general hospitals; preventive and educational services in settings such as libraries, churches, and hospital waiting rooms; screening and early intervention programs in public schools; crisis intervention and telephone hot lines; and greater use of home care.

This range of services is girded by a set of beliefs that reflect a democratic orientation to mental health services and a social systems perspective on change. According to these beliefs, mental health services are a public utility and a civil right, rather than a service available only to those individuals who possess adequate finances or insurance. In addition, individuals for whom these services are intended should retain personal freedom and make decisions regarding the use of resources.[28] Finally, because the *method* of service delivery is believed to be as important as the nature of the service, the community mental health movement maintains that change must be planned for, be systematic, and be aimed at social systems, such as schools, organizations, industry, or families, rather than at individuals,[1,11,28] and that prevention and early intervention are more desirable than later intervention and treatment.[11]

Prevention can occur on three levels. *Primary prevention* aims at the reduction of incidence or occurrence of disorder through two main strategies: modifying environments and strengthening people's coping abilities. Neither of these strategies is carried out on an individual level. The first is accomplished by analyzing social systems and intervening at this level. For example, developing special high school programs that combine community work with academic classes is a social systems intervention directed at the educational environment. The second strategy is achieved through consultation to schools and churches, to programs for at-risk populations (such as children of divorced parents or families of people who are terminally ill), and to individuals who work with large groups of people (the clergy, for instance).[9] *Secondary prevention* involves early detection of problems, through such means as educating the public and ensuring that services are available to and used by individuals. Thus, although the occurrence of the problem is not eliminated by this level of prevention, the problem is minimized by early identification and treatment. Finally, *tertiary prevention* is concerned with eliminating or reducing the impact of problems by returning individuals to productive community roles and preventing further recurrences.[9]

Another emphasis in community mental health is intervention that is directed at groups. Groups are more economical, and through approaches such as family and network therapy, complete social systems within a community can be influenced.[9] Network therapy is an interesting development in community group treatment. The network therapist, labeled "conductor," collects as many different people as possible who know the identified client. These people may range from family members and close friends to persons working in the community with whom the client has contact. This enables examination of the person's problems in all sectors of daily life. All members of the network are then involved in formulating and enacting solutions to the problems.[9]

Community mental health programs have fostered a reconsideration of the traditional role of the professional. In part, the situation has been one of professionals changing their role in *reaction* to the increased use of indigenous and paraprofessional workers. The use of nonprofessionals, such as teachers' aides, childcare workers, psychiatric aides, parents, students, and so on, has been found to have beneficial effects on both the helper and client, because the helper is seen as a competent role model.[12] In addition, social support from a peer may have more immediate and personal value to the recipient than more clinically oriented treatment provided by a professional.[11] Nontraditional work roles have also been seen as providing a way of bringing groups of people who are traditionally outside the cultural mainstream—and thus at risk for disorder—into it.[11] As nonprofessional personnel have been used to provide primary intervention, or direct care, the professional has had to broaden his or her role to encompass staff training, supervision, consulting, program development, and evaluation.[12]

Professional roles have changed *proactively* as well as reactively. An example is the involvement of professionals in the development of mass media programs for radio, television, newspapers, and film designed to educate the public about preventive, healthful life-styles.[12]

Along with alternative work roles and careers, the last major action implication in this movement is the creation of alternative institutions. These new institutions have most commonly been alternatives to traditional schooling, to incarceration of criminals, and to long-term residential treatment of psychosocially disordered people. The purposes of these new settings have generally been to return deviants to mainstream society or, particularly in the case of schools, to maximize the match between a person's needs and what the setting provides.[11] For psychiatric clients these alternatives to hospitalization include board-and-care homes, day programs emphasizing the development of vocational and recreational skills, and halfway houses designed to bridge the transition from institution to community.[11,12,14]

CRITICISMS AND LIMITATIONS

The reality of community mental health is not as innovative or exciting as the ideal picture that has been portrayed. To a great extent, the failures of this movement stem from its inability to separate from traditional American medicine. In a sense, the movement was doomed from the very beginning when the original Community Mental Health Centers Act stated its intent to "return mental health care to the mainstream of American medicine" (p. 185).[12] This immediately tied the movement to the medical model.

The first problem arising from the link to the medical model was that the original services mandated by the government were traditional clinical services, or the things psychiatrists were "good at."[12] Delineating and requiring these traditional services precluded or slowed the development of innovative services and made more difficult the use of nonprofessional workers. When the latter were used, having to fit into the hierarchical structure of the medical model created conflicts around decision making, discrimination, career-advancement opportunities, and working relationships in general. The one nonclinical service that was mandated by the initial act and which did not derive from the medical model—consultation and education—was intended as an adjunct to clinical services, and not to change social institutions.[12] In addition, this service was the least consistently enacted.[4] Through this early medical model dominance, the potential for social innovation that many hoped for from the movement was severely limited.

The original act implicitly designated long-term hospitalization as bad, contributing to a lasting polarization between community mental health personnel and hospital personnel.[4] Further, the act created a need for local, state, and federal governments to work interdependently and for the federal government to assume responsibility for equalizing affluence across states.[4] With hindsight we can see that this has left the poorer states in a vulnerable position as federal monies have become scarcer.

Another problem stemming from the original act is that it derived from a belief in the benevolence of both government and medical professionals. Interestingly, the original enthusiasm and trust in government and professionals' efforts to manipulate the environment in order to promote mental health has changed to distrust and skepticism.[17] The climate of our country currently does not favor a strong governmental role, and individuals seem wary of sociological and legal interpretations of mental illness. Psychiatrists, if not yet wary, may soon be, as they are now becoming frequent victims of violent "patients."[23] Insanity as a legal defense is less popular and has been banned in some states altogether; this too seems to be a reflection of a more generalized dissatisfaction with the role of mental health professionals in the community in its implication that psychiatrists cannot and should not determine when crime is truly the product of insanity.

Recently, criticism of the process of deinstitutionalization has surfaced. Although the overall hospital population has decreased, the number of admissions has not, and it is felt that this is largely because the community centers have not offered support services and follow-up care to discharged clients. Many board-and-care homes and halfway houses, which were presumably created to offer these services, have turned out instead to be back wards in the community where the typical resident spends most "of the day in virtual solitude, either staring vacantly at television . . . or wandering aimlessly around the neighborhood" (pp. 461–462).[25] These residential facilities have frequently become entrepreneurial, profit-making operations that see residents as commodities to be obtained and controlled.[13] Further, many clients have been prematurely "dumped" without adequate preparation for community living.[20] The too-frequent result has been that deinstitutionalized people have not become a part of the community in any real sense.[13,20]

Finally, although the community mental health movement was guided by the belief that the source of disorder was in the community, many critics feel that it actually succeeded only in relabeling social problems as psychiatric problems instead of pinpointing social determinants of psychological problems.[12]

COMMENTARY

Many of the most innovative and exciting programs to be developed in the community have developed, unfortunately, without occupational therapists; yet these programs offer social and daily living skills training, prevocational training, and leisure programs. Occupational therapists who *have* moved along into the community have often too willingly adopted the roles created for them by other mental health workers already there. For instance, Schechter[20] describes a psychiatric day program in which the occupational therapist assumed the role established by the psychiatrist and social worker and became a primary therapist, coordinating treatment for assigned patients, working with families, participating in group therapy, and providing psychodynamically oriented occupational therapy groups. While the role of counselor and case coordinator may be interesting and important, it may not be the one for which the occupational therapist is best suited. On the other hand, Broekema, Danz, and Schloemer[6] describe a more suitable occupational therapy role in a community aftercare program where occupational therapy provided basic living skills and job finding skills groups, and an arts and crafts group in which members were able to experience feelings of competence and pleasure during leisure. Also capitalizing on the strengths of occupational therapy, Auerbach,[3] along with a client from a day treatment center, joined the Bernal Heights Ladies' Club. Becoming a regular member enabled her to help ease the transition for other clients into community groups and to help community members accept psychiatric clients into their group. Working with a psychologist and a management consultant in the early seventies, Dunning[8] presaged an important role for occupational therapists in collaborative job training programs for psychotic people, but the area of consultancy to industry on job adaptation, relocation problems of living, and balancing leisure and work meaningfully and with satisfaction to the individual has yet to be exploited by occupational therapists.[22] Bockoven,[5] a psychiatrist, suggests that the future of the community mental health movement lies with occupational therapists, who must assume the role of occupational developers for the community:

> A new era of moral treatment tailored to our times is sorely needed not only by thousands of persons in our communities who are burdened with chronic residues of psychoses, but also by many thousands of others with emotional and physical limitations.
>
> It is fair to say that modern society has a greater need for comprehensive community occupational-recreational programs than it has for mental health centers. . . . Similarly, I would like to suggest that occupational therapy be the wellspring for a sorely needed alternative system of education for individuals of all ages for whom the formal public school system, as we know it today, is inadequate. (pp. 224–225)[5]

As Wiemer,[26] Laukaran,[15] and other writers note, occupational therapists already possess the knowledge and skills to be unique and important participants in the community mental health movement. Whether or not we become successful in this role may yet depend on our willingness to reassess the importance of the disparate strands of knowledge we still claim as vital to our work. The importance of this role, as part of our function as environmental managers, will be further elaborated in the second part of this text.

SUMMARY

History and Purpose	The rapid growth of institutions and an organic view of disorder led to an increasingly custodial emphasis in treatment in late 19th century.
	Various reformers proposed establishment of community mental hygiene districts.
	In the 1950s biochemical treatment led to the discharge of many chronically ill people from large institutions.
	Under President Kennedy, a Community Mental Health Centers Act was proposed to improve inpatient and outpatient services and to change public attitudes toward mental illness.
View of Order	As an interdisciplinary, politically based movement, the view of order is not well articulated.
	Emphases include a belief in the importance of interpersonal relationships (particularly the family unit), a competence view of health, and belief in the necessity for developing social support systems that promote health.
View of Disorder	Disorder arises from a number of factors: genetic, constitutional, developmental, and environmental.
	The present-day social structure has also contributed to disorder, through the alienation of individuals from their work and communities, through conflicting values in modern life, and factors such as crowding and the fast pace of life.

Action Implications	A focus on prevention and early intervention is the cornerstone of the movement.
	Three levels of prevention exist: *primary* concerns modifying environments and people's coping abilities so that the incidence of disorder is reduced; *secondary* involves early detection of problems; and *tertiary* aims to reduce the impact of problems.
	Intervention tends to be directed at groups and social systems rather than individuals.
	The increasing use of nonprofessionals has led to changing roles for professionals.
	Many alternative "institutions" have been created.
Criticisms and Limitations	Community mental health has been dominated by the medical model, which has limited its potential for social innovation.
	The movement created a polarization between mental health workers in hospital settings and those in the community.
	Many of the alternative treatment settings established in the community do no more for their residents than long-term institutions did.
Commentary	Although occupational therapists clearly have a place in community treatment, they have frequently assumed the roles created by other mental health workers instead of capitalizing on their own strengths.
	Bockoven suggests that the future of community mental health lies with occupational therapists.

TERMS AND CONCEPTS

action model of mental illness	a model that emphasizes treatment strategies and courses of intervention.
catchment area	geographically defined region to which a particular community mental health center offers services.

157

causal model of mental illness	a model concerned with conceptualizing the origins or formation of mental illness.
multifactorial view of disorder	a perspective that identifies many sources (or factors) as contributing to pathology, rather than one cause.
primary prevention	strategies that seek to prevent the occurrence of disorder, e.g., environmental modification and programs for "at-risk" individuals.
proactive	making changes in anticipation of future needs as opposed to changing in response to some event or some need that has already been identified.
secondary prevention	early detection of problems, accomplished through public education and increased availability of services, so that the impact of problems is diminished.
tertiary prevention	minimization of the effects of pathology, by enabling people to return to productive community roles after illness.

REFERENCES

1. Adelson, D. A concept of comprehensive community mental health. In D. Adelson & B. L. Kalis (Eds.), *Community psychology and mental health.* Scranton, Pa.: Chadler, 1970.
2. Albee, G. W. A competency model of health to replace the defect model. In M. S. Gibbs, J. R. Lachenmeyer, & J. Sigal (Eds.), *Community psychology.* New York: Gardner Press, 1980.
3. Auerbach, E. Community involvement: The Bernal Heights Ladies' Club. *American Journal of Occupational Therapy,* 1974, *28,* 272–273.
4. Bloom, B. L. *Community mental health: A general introduction.* Monterey, Calif.: Brooks/Cole, 1977.
5. Bockoven, J. S. *Moral treatment in community mental health.* New York: Springer, 1972.
6. Broekema, M. C., Danz, K. H., & Schloemer, C. U. Occupational therapy in a community aftercare program. *American Journal of Occupational Therapy,* 1975, *28,* 22–27.
7. Cohen, L. D. Health and disease: Observations on strategies for community psychology. In G. Rosenblum (Ed.), *Issues in community psychology and preventive mental health.* New York: Behavioral Publications, 1971.
8. Deacon, S., Dunning, R. E., & Dease, R. A job clinic for psychotic

clients in remission. *American Journal of Occupational Therapy*, 1974, *28*, 144–147.

9. Gottesfeld, H. *Abnormal psychology: A community mental health perspective.* Chicago: Science Research Associates, 1979.

10. Grob, G. N. *Mental institutions in America: Social policy to 1875.* New York: Free Press, 1973.

11. Heller, K., & Monahan, J. *Psychology and community change.* Homewood, Ill.: Dorsey, 1977.

12. Jeger, A. M. Community mental health and environmental design. In L. Krasner (Ed.), *A psychology of the individual in society.* New York: Pergamon Press, 1980.

13. Kielhofner, G. An ethnographic study of deinstitutionalized adults. *Occupational Therapy Journal of Research*, 1981, *1*, 125–142.

14. Lamb, H. R., and associates. *Community survival for long-term patients.* San Francisco: Jossey-Bass, 1976.

15. Laukaran, V. H. Nationally speaking—Toward a model of occupational therapy for community health. *American Journal of Occupational Therapy*, 1977, *31*, 71–74.

16. Magaro, P., Gripp, R., McDowell, D. J., & Miller, I. W. III. *The mental health industry: A cultural phenomenon.* New York: Wiley, 1978.

17. Musto, D. F. The community mental health movement in historical perspective. In W. E. Barton & C. J. Sanborn (Eds.), *An assessment of the community mental health movement.* Lexington, Mass.: Lexington Books, 1975.

18. Ozarin, L. D. Community mental health: Does it work? Review of the evaluation. In W. E. Barton & C. J. Sanborn (Eds.), *An assessment of the community mental health movement.* Lexington, Mass.: Lexington Books, 1975.

19. Panzetta, A. F. *Community mental health: Myth and reality.* Philadelphia: Lea & Febiger, 1971.

20. Schechter, L. Occupational therapy in a psychiatric day hospital. *American Journal of Occupational Therapy*, 1974, *28*, 151–153.

21. Scull, A. T. *Decarceration: Community treatment and the deviant—A radical view.* Englewood Cliffs, N.J.: Prentice-Hall, 1977.

22. Sigal, J. Physical environment stressors. In M. S. Gibbs, J. R. Lachenmeyer, & J. Sigal (Eds.), *Community psychology.* New York: Gardner Press, 1980.

23. Sorenson, J. Nationally speaking—Occupational therapy in business: A new horizon. *American Journal of Occupational Therapy*, 1978, *32*, 287–288.

24. Szasz, T. Shooting the shrink. *New Republic*, June 16, 1982, *186*, pp. 11, 13–14.
25. Van Putten, T., & Spar, J. E. The board-and-care home: Does it deserve bad press? *Hospital and Community Psychiatry*, 1979, *30*, 461–464.
26. Wiemer, R. B. Some concepts of prevention as an aspect of community health. *American Journal of Occupational Therapy*, 1972, *26*, 1–9.
27. Zautra, A., & Simons, L. S. Some effects of positive life events on community mental health. *American Journal of Community Psychology*, 1979, *7*, 441–451.
28. Zax, M. History and background of the community mental health movement. In M. S. Gibbs, J. R. Lachenmeyer, & J. Sigal (Eds.), *Community psychology*. New York: Gardner Press, 1980.
29. Zusman, J. The philosophic basis for a community and social psychiatry. In W. E. Barton & C. J. Sanborn (Eds.), *An assessment of the community mental health movement*. Lexington, Mass.: Lexington Books, 1975.

ADDITIONAL READINGS

Barton, W. E., & Sanborn, C. J. (Eds.). *An assessment of the community mental health movement*. Lexington, Mass.: Lexington Books, 1975.

Borus, J. F. Issues critical to the survival of community mental health. *American Journal of Psychiatry*, 1978, *135*, 1029–1034.

Butz, C. W. *A study of the roles of the O.T. in community mental health programs*. Unpublished thesis, University of Nebraska, 1969.

Conte, W. R., & Meuli, A. L. Occupational therapy in community mental health. *American Journal of Occupational Therapy*, 1966, *20*, 147–150.

Howe, M., & Dippy, K. The role of occupational therapy in community mental health. *American Journal of Occupational Therapy*, 1968, *22*, 521–524.

Iscoe, I., Bloom, B. L., & Spielberger, C. D. *Community psychology in transition: Proceedings of the National Conference on Training in Community Psychology*. Washington, D.C.: Hemisphere Publishing Corp., 1977.

Levine, M. *The history and politics of community mental health*. New York: Oxford University Press, 1981.

11
Deviance or Labeling Theory

Deviance or labeling theory, a sociocultural tradition of thought, seeks to explain the social processes that occur when persons deviate from the ordinary ethos of daily life. Erikson[6] defines deviance as:

> conduct which is generally thought to require the attention of social control agencies—that is, conduct about which "something should be done." Deviance is not a property *inherent in* certain forms of behavior; it is a property *conferred upon* these forms by audiences which directly or indirectly witness them. (p. 11)

As this definition illustrates, deviance involves a concatenation of actions and reactions. This tradition argues that persons labeled mentally ill or retarded violate social rules, evoking the judgments and actions of others and creating a situation of social deviance. Psychosocial dysfunction is one of many forms of deviant behavior studied by social scientists.

Deviance theory is of particular interest to the clinician since, unlike many other explanations of psychosocial dysfunction, it does not locate the "problem" entirely within the person who has an emotional or cognitive difficulty. Strictly speaking, it is not a theory of psychosocial dysfunction, but a theory about its underlying social processes.

HISTORY AND PURPOSE

The study of deviance arose within the fields of sociology and anthropology. It reflects their classic concern with the structures and processes of group life. The study of deviant persons, their aberrations, and societal reactions to them provides a perspective for understanding how society maintains its ordered character.[1] Initially, social scientists focused on deviants themselves, detailing their characteristics, practices, and life-styles. However, the topic of more recent work is the interactive process between "normals" and deviants.[1] Concern has shifted from how the deviant transgresses social rules of conduct to how deviance is created not only through rule breaking but by social response. Social scientists study how both everyday cultural members and organized institutions and professionals respond to and act toward the deviant person.[2,3]

According to recent concepts of social groups as integrated systems that maintain their own boundaries, deviance is a process of social self-control.[6] Deviant behavior appears to have a paradoxical relationship to social processes. On the one hand, deviants are threats to the ongoing order since they violate social norms. At the same time, they constitute an important source of information to other members about what behavior is out of bounds. Consequently, it is argued that society needs its deviants as means of demarcating social boundaries. For instance, mentally ill and retarded persons are recognized foremost as individuals who violate social norms. They are, therefore, responded to in predictable ways by everyday cultural members and by socially approved agents and agencies of control. At the same time, they enable society to advertise and maintain its concepts of sanity and appropriate behavior.

VIEW OF ORDER

The social science concepts underlying deviance theory present order as the result of interaction between persons and their social surroundings. Participation by the individual in the ongoing processes of social life yields a view of self and of society.[2,4] This view comprises both the person's and society's beliefs about reality and provides personal guidelines for social actions. It includes such elements as the values and norms of society and recognition of roles and their related behavior. Thus, the social participant, in each encounter with others, is acting out a view of reality that he or she acquires from society. The individual is shaped and defined by social processes to conform to the values, norms, and other expectations of the social group.

At the same time, social life itself consists of individuals interacting with each other, employing their respective views of reality. As they interact, they continually reshape each others' views and, thus, construct ongoing reality.[3] Social life and its patterned order is, then, a system of interacting viewpoints and behaviors. Collectively, social actors constitute and create the reality of everyday life as they participate in it.

Of particular relevance to the situation of deviance is the social science concept that what persons become is a function of complex social interactions. Goode[9] refers to this process as sociogenic identity. By this he means that persons eventually behave as others expect them to and see themselves as others see them. One's identity is thus a function of one's social surroundings. Everyone has experienced this phenomenon in a small way when entering new social situations. Individuals may have thought of themselves, and have been viewed in the past, as having a great sense of humor or the ability to give good personal advice. In a new situation, one may find that it is not so easy to tell a joke or offer advice in the same manner as one did in the old familiar setting. There is typically a "warming up" period in which one slowly and gradually offers such behaviors geared to shape others' impressions toward one's view of self. As one's own and others' views become similar in their expectations, one can more freely and frequently engage in old humorous or advice-giving behaviors. On the other hand, if those in the new setting do not find one funny or wise, one may come to doubt one's own abilities. As the example illustrates, the individual and society (both consciously and automatically) shape each other. The order of social life and the order of the individual's identity and behavior result from this mutually influential process.

VIEW OF DISORDER

Several currents of thought characterize social science explanations of the processes that underlie becoming and being deviant. Classically, social scientists, attempting to counteract the popular cultural notion that deviance was an undesirable property of the individual, portrayed the deviant as reacting to intolerable or troubled social conditions.[6] The deviant person was often romanticized as a folk hero. The image of the mentally ill person as highly sensitive to the insanity of the world at large is an example of this orientation. More recent views of deviance recognize that attributes leading up to the violation of social convention (i.e., emotional and intellectual disturbances) may be properties in the individual, but they emphasize that the recognition or attribution of deviant status (for it is the construction of deviant status which most concerns social scientists) is an interactive process involving both the deviant's behavior and social response.[2]

Thus, the deviant phenomenon is a complementary process of rule breaking by the deviant, and recognition and attribution of deviant status to the rule-breaker by members of society.[1] In this sense, deviant identity (including mental illness) is socially constructed reality. This view stresses that the deviance is not merely a quality inherent in the person, but the result of social processes involving interaction of social members. This has led naturally to an increased focus on those who interact with the deviant, especially those who officially define and attempt to control deviant behavior.

Identifying and Labeling Deviance

Because social reaction to rule infraction is recognized as an essential component of deviance, the problem of differential definition and reaction to behavior is important. For example, since behaviors are labeled and reacted to differently over time, the same act may be labeled or not labeled as a deviant performance.[1] A simple example is society's negative reaction to the long hair worn by males in the 1960s and 1970s by a society whose religious and civil symbols include ample protrayal of men from other eras who also wore long hair.

The particular social institution given responsibility for controlling a form of deviance will define the deviant act according to its own concerns and methods. For example, when religious institutions attempt to control homosexuality, they define it as sin. Several years ago, when psychiatry attempted control of homosexual behavior it defined homosexuality as an illness. When legislative bodies attempt control, they define homosexuality as a crime. Thus, the deviant may be considered immoral, diseased, and/or criminal depending on the institution that attempts to control the deviance.

In addition, societal views may be varied so that social institutions are no longer required to control a behavior once considered deviant. For example, in many communities and among many heterosexuals, homosexuality is now considered a normal life-style option. If such an opinion is accepted by a majority of society, social institutions such as churches, prisons, and mental health professionals will find no reason to condemn, treat, or punish such behavior. What this also illustrates is that deviance is less an inherent property of any behavior than it is a property of the social groups that react to and attempt to control it.

Deviance theory offers an important perspective on the arbitrary nature of current psychiatric practice. It has been pointed out that values embedded in modern psychiatry represent the current ideology of middle class Western society.[17] One important set of observations on the indeterminacy of modern psychiatric procedures demonstrates that the process of identifying or labeling mental illness can be highly inaccurate. Studies have shown that a plethora of elements can influence the outcome of a psychiatric diagnostic procedure, resulting in disagreements between different diagnosticians or changes in a person's view of someone's mental problem over time.[12] In a dramatic study, a group of social scientists and graduate students were admitted covertly to various psychiatric wards as "psychotic patients." None of the mental health personnel detected or even suspected the sanity or true identity of these persons. The fact of their hospitalization and the label of mental illness overruled all other evidence and maintained their social identities as mental patients.[15]

Thus, deviance theory emphasizes that human identities are not only a feature of inherent characteristics, but also are a function of social values, definitions, and expectations that are guiding elements of human interactions in which deviance is created. It stresses the arbitrary nature of many social judgments and, thus, offers a more humanistic perspective of the deviant person.

Intensifying and Perpetuating Deviance

Some sociologists argue that society unnecessarily labels certain kinds of personal traits and behaviors as deviant,[5,7] and that the actions of those charged with managing deviants actually intensify and maintain deviant behavior.[2,18] This concept, often referred to as "labeling theory," stresses the role of societal reaction in augmenting the deviant career of those labeled as mentally ill or mentally retarded. According to this view, the person with psychosocial dysfunction violates social rules, is subsequently recognized as having a problem, and receives the ministrations of persons and institutions (e.g., institutionalization and therapy). As a result of these social responses, the person with psychosocial dysfunction acquires both an internal and external deviant identity. That is, such persons come to view themselves as possessing certain undesirable qualities, they come to view others who are likewise labeled as undesirable, and they are in turn recognized and treated by others as undesirable. This may result in the deviance becoming permanent or more pronounced. For example, a study of retarded persons demonstrated that those labeled intellectually subnormal fared better in the long run if their families rejected the retarded label. Those whose families accepted the label apparently fared worse, since they were more likely to view themselves and to be treated by others as mentally defective.[13]

Goffman[8] documented what he called the "moral career" of the mental patient. He argued that there are effects of social processes separate from any pathological disturbance in the mentally ill person. He points out that, while persons who become mental patients vary widely in their personalities, symptoms, and underlying pathology, they come to have a common deviant identity and exhibit similar deviant behavior. He attributes this to the experience of hospitalization and the treatment of persons labeled as mentally ill. Goffman explains that people who are mentally ill enter into a process of self-redefinition that is directed by the social circumstances of hospitalization and results in many of the apparently asocial features associated with psychosocial disorder. Paradoxically, those institutions whose purpose is to control or eliminate deviance instead yield their own special brand of deviance.

Thus, deviance theories recognize that while the etiology of mental illness or retardation may have biological and psychological roots, it also has an identifiable social genesis. Erikson[6] describes this as follows:

> The community's decision to bring deviant sanctions against an individual is not a simple act of censure. It is a sharp rite of transition, at once moving him out of his normal position in society and transferring him to a distinct deviant role. The ceremonies which accomplish this change of status, ordinarily have three related phases. They provide a formal *confrontation* between the deviant suspect

and representatives of his community (as in the criminal trial or psychiatric case conference); they announce some *judgment* about the nature of his deviancy (a verdict or diagnosis, for example); and they perform an act of social placement, assigning him to a special role (like that of a prisoner or patient) which redefines his position in society. (p. 16)

The process of labeling may intensify deviance through the self-fulfilling prophecy, since deviant persons are typically expected to retain some element of their deviance permanently. For instance, a common expectation is that the person who was once mentally ill will always possess a weak or deficient personality. Such expectations make it difficult for the deviant to reenter society (e.g., to find jobs after having been hospitalized for mental illness). As a result, labels often create the reality they assume. For example, the expectation that people who were once mentally ill are poor job prospects adds to their difficulties in developing sound job histories.[6]

Stigma

Another aspect of deviance theory's contribution to explaining psychosocial problems is the concept of stigma. Goffman[8] borrows the term stigma from the Greek word that referred to individuals marked (by disfigurement) for their offenses against society. Goffman defines stigmatized individuals as persons who bear a psychological or physical trait that makes them stand apart from the average cultural member of any setting. As Goffman[8] notes, the one pervasive law of all social settings is that people must fit in. Those who are different, who do not fit in, who are noticeable by virtue of their nonconforming traits, are stigmatized.

The stigmatized individual is perceived and treated as though he or she were not quite human.[8] Stigmatized persons are viewed as bad, undesirable, dangerous, or weak. According to Goffman there are three different types of stigma: abominations of the body; the tribal stigma of race, nationality, and religion; and blemishes of individual character, which include mental illness and mental retardation.

What is important about stigmatized individuals is that their "virtual social identity" (i.e., that identity imputed to them by virtue of the stigmatizing characteristic) overrides an actual identity. Ordinary human foibles and limitations are often construed as a function of the stigmatizing characteristic. For example, if a "normal" person forgets to take change from a cashier and begins to walk away only to be called back, his or her mistake is recognized as just that—a mistake due to being absentminded or preoccupied at the moment. It is seen as a situational act that does not reflect on the person's real identity. If, however, a retarded person commits the same error, one's tendency is to construe the act as, first, the result of the retardation and, second, evidence of the problematic nature of the retardation. Thought processes related to stigma can thus make pathological mountains out of the molehills of common human error.

In summary, deviance theory illustrates much of the complex social dynamics that accompany and affect psychosocial dysfunction. Deviance or labeling theory is not an attempt to explain the original cause of a person's deviant behavior, rather, it illuminates important social processes that influence the experience, behavior, and identity of the deviant person.[2]

ACTION IMPLICATIONS

Deviance or labeling theory does not provide guidelines for action on an individual basis. Instead, it provides a framework for reexamining traditional assumptions or approaches to therapy. Social scientists have often taken a pessimistic view of therapeutic enterprises, emphasizing that systems and persons charged with care and control of deviants oppress them and augment their deviance. The term "moral entrepreneurs" is used to characterize those who devote their life efforts to pursuing and correcting a certain genre of deviance.[1] Therapy is often looked on as a process more oriented to maintaining social reality at large than to ameliorating individuals' problems, because it attempts to eliminate behaviors that threaten the legitimacy of mainstream values, ideas, practices, and rules.[3,5]

While much of the sociological literature does paint a negative view of therapeutic efforts, some writers stress that positive effects can result when therapeutic endeavors take into consideration the need for positive socialization of the deviant.[16] This means that therapy must offer persons with psychosocial dysfunction access to legitimate roles in society. Further, they must be viewed in terms of their commonality with others instead of being treated as outcasts.

Deviance or labeling theories should not be seen as nihilistic statements on therapy, but as providing useful guidelines for avoiding processes that unwittingly socialize patients into permanent deviant roles or intensify deviance. In general, deviance theory suggests that therapy should not remove the mentally ill person from mainstream society and that all therapeutic efforts that necessarily involve removal should focus on maintaining ties with and roles in social life. A final theme is that social change must accompany more humanistic approaches to psychosocial problems. More enlightened attitudes and greater tolerance and understanding of deviant behavior will be needed to avoid the negative effects that can occur from social reaction to the deviant person.

CRITICISMS AND LIMITATIONS

Criticisms of deviant perspectives come from two opposite directions.[2] On the one hand, critics propose that deviance perspectives have often overlooked the undesirability or pathology of the deviant act. Others propose that deviant perspectives have not fully accounted for the oppression that social systems impose on their members as manifest in reactions to deviants. Becker[2] argues that the purpose of social science views of deviance was to accomplish neither of these objectives, but rather to document the processes involved in the deviant status.

It remains that deviance perspectives offer only partial accounts of what happens to mentally ill people or what constitutes psychosocial disorder. This is offered not as a criticism but as a statement on the scope of deviance theory and its relationship to the problem of psychosocial disorder. While biological or psychological etiology and processes are not accounted for in this perspective, it does offer important insights into the social processes surrounding reaction to and management of those who have a psychosocial dysfunction.

COMMENTARY

The deviance perspective enhances understanding of how the processes of therapy can affect the career of the hospitalized person. Reilly[14] acknowledged the theme that hospitalization can intensify the deviant pattern by negatively affecting the occupational skills and roles that individuals need for community life. She suggested organizing occupational therapy as a socializing process that assumes responsibility for maintaining these occupational roles and skills. In therapy, the person should be treated in terms of social expectations and rewards for performance of normal life tasks.[10,11]

Goode[9] has pointed out how, in occupational therapy as in other health disciplines, clinical evaluation procedures can be unnecessarily fault-finding in their orientation. Such assessment does more to stigmatize people's identities than to suggest any clear directions for treatment. He argues that assessment procedures must meet deviant people on their own terms and reflect the ways in which individuals would view their own behaviors and life circumstances.

The deviance perspective is instructive in pointing out how treatment or therapy is always a process of negotiating between viewpoints and over what is proper, acceptable, and worthy of learning. For occupational therapists to socialize individuals into those perspectives and practices that are deemed more competent from the dominant cultural perspective, they must be sensitive to the person's own viewpoints and common sense. Therapy should be a way of bridging the gap, of making the desired social behavior acceptable and meaningful to the person.

Occupational therapy is particularly suited to this process since it has a long tradition of providing action contexts in which individuals can opt to try out and experience socially approved behaviors in various situations. Thus, while therapy does serve the purpose of reducing or controlling deviance, it can do so in a manner that gives the deviant person a reason to choose and enact adaptive behavior.

SUMMARY

History and Purpose	Deviance or labeling theory is part of the social science concern for the structures and processes of group life.
	Early studies romanticized the deviant as a martyr of a disturbed society.
	Current views focus on the interactions between the deviant and society and the role of the deviant in maintaining the boundaries of society.
View of Order	Order results from the interaction of the person and social environment.
	The individual's view of reality and behavior is shaped by the values and norms that society provides.
	Society is maintained and created through the interactions of its members.
View of Disorder	Psychosocial disorder is recognized as deviance—a situation in which people violate rules of society and are identified and responded to as rule-breakers.
	Social control agents and agencies may intensify and perpetuate deviance.
	Because of societal reaction, the deviant's identity (as a deviant) undergoes a transformation (e.g., the moral career of mental patients, acquisition of stigma).
Action Implications	Some social scientists are pessimistic about therapeutic efforts, but others recognize that when therapists are sensitive to the deviance process and seek positive socialization experiences, therapy can benefit people.

Criticisms and Limitations	Deviance theory has been criticized for underrating either the deviant's pathological behavior or the degree to which society oppresses the deviant. Actually, deviance theory seeks to describe the interactions between the deviant person and society without creating blame for either.
Commentary	Therapists should be sensitive to their own attitudes and actions toward the deviant person, taking care to focus on healthy aspects of behavior and the deviant's humanity.
	Positive socialization experiences can be developed so that occupational therapy is an arena where social expectations and individual perspectives can profitably be brought into interaction.

TERMS AND CONCEPTS

asocial	showing no awareness or regard for society's definitions of appropriate behavior.
moral career	a process of self-redefinition in which the institutionalized person receives a new identity as a subhuman entity and learns to behave as a chronic patient.
moral entrepreneur	a person who takes it upon him- or herself to identify people with a type of deviance and who seeks to control it.
norms	implicit and explicit expectations of society for how its members should behave; norms generally pertain to one's age, life, role, and the particular subgroup to which one belongs.
social control	any process that seeks to limit or change behavior of those who violate social rules.
social rules	a process whereby people interacting with a social group come to take on its attitudes and beliefs and to conform their behavior to the rules and norm of the group.

sociogenic   arising from or caused by social factors.

stigma   a physical, mental, and/or emotional trait that is
                identified by others as being inferior, bad, flawed,
                or otherwise undesirable. A person with a stigma is
                identified through the stigma (e.g., one is a "cripple,"
                a "crazy").

REFERENCES

1. Becker, H. S. (Ed.). *The other side: Perspectives on deviance*. New York: Free Press, 1964.
2. Becker, H. S. *Outsiders: Studies in the sociology of deviance*. New York: Free Press, 1973.
3. Berger, P. L., & Luckman, T. *The social construction of reality*. New York: Anchor Books, 1967.
4. Blumer, H. *Symbolic interactionism: Perspective and method*. Englewood Cliffs, N.J.: Prentice-Hall, 1969.
5. Dexter, L. A. On the politics and sociology of stupidity in our society. In H. S. Becker (Ed.), *The other side: Perspectives on deviance*. New York: Free Press, 1964.
6. Erikson, K. T. Notes on the sociology of deviance. In H. S. Becker (Ed.), *The other side: Perspectives on deviance*. New York: Free Press, 1973.
7. Freidson, E. Disability as social deviance. In E. Freidson & J. Lorber (Eds.), *Medical men and their work: A sociological reader*. Chicago: Aldine-Atherton, 1972.
8. Goffman, E. *Asylums*. New York: Anchor Books, 1961.
9. Goode, D. Who is Bobby? Ideology and method in the discovery of a Down's Syndrome person's competence. In G. Kielhofner (Ed.), *Health through occupation: Theory and practice in occupational therapy*. Philadelphia: F. A. Davis, 1983.
10. Kielhofner, G. The temporal dimension in the lives of retarded adults. *American Journal of Occupational Therapy*, 1979, *33*, 161–168.
11. Kielhofner, G., & Takata, N. A study of mentally retarded persons: Applied research in occupational therapy. *American Journal of Occupational Therapy*, 1980, *34*, 252–258.
12. Mehan, H., & Wood, H. *The reality of ethnomethology*. New York: John Wiley and Sons, 1975.
13. Mercer, J. Career patterns of persons labeled as mentally retarded. In E. Friedson & J. Lorber (Eds.), *Medical men and their work: A sociological reader*. Chicago: Aldine-Atherton, 1972.

14. Reilly, M. A psychiatric occupational therapy program as a teaching model. *American Journal of Occupational Therapy*, 1966, *20*, 61–67.

15. Rosenhan, On being sane in insane places. In T. J. Scheff (Ed.), *Labeling madness*. Englewood Cliffs, N.J.: Prentice-Hall, 1975.

16. Samson, H., & Messinger, S. The mental hospital and marital family ties. In H. S. Becker (Ed.), *The other side: Perspectives on deviance*. New York: Free Press, 1964.

17. Scheff, T. J. *Labeling madness*. Englewood Cliffs, N.J.: Prentice-Hall, 1975.

18. Zusman, J. Some explanations of the changing appearance of psychotic patients. In R. H. Price & B. Denner (Eds.), *The making of a mental patient*. New York: Holt, Rinehart & Winston, 1973.